100 ideas for today's chicken

microwave cooking library®

by barbara methven

microwave cooking library®

Almost everybody eats chicken. It's tasty, nutritious and economical. Naturally lean, chicken combines well with vegetables, fruits and grains to create today's healthy, low-fat, high-fiber meals. If you're looking for new ways to fix this favorite, you'll welcome *100 Ideas for Today's Chicken.*

The book features quick-idea pages to introduce each section. They present simple, basic preparation techniques, then provide ideas for several totally different ways to use them. To complete the sections, plenty of delicious recipes plus more quick-and-easy ideas make chicken exciting.

You don't have to be on a budget or a diet to enjoy chicken. This book gives you recipes to suit every taste. Flavor your chicken subtle or spicy, homey or exotic; it's so versatile you can serve it a different way every day of the week.

Barbara Methven

Barbara Methven

CREDITS:
Design & Production: Cy DeCosse Incorporated
Art Directors: Mark Jacobson, David Schelitzche, Lori Swanson
Project Director: Peggy Ramette
Project Managers: Deborah Bialik, Diane Dreon-Krattiger
Home Economists: Bonnie Ellingboe, Virginia A. Hoeschen, Ellen Meis, Peggy Ramette, Ann Stuart, Grace Wells
Dietitian: Hill Nutrition Associates, Inc.
Consultants: Susanne Mattison, Grace Wells
Editor: Janice Cauley
Director of Development Planning & Production: Jim Bindas
Production Manager: Amelia Merz
Electronic Publishing Specialist: Joe Fahey
Production Staff: Adam Esco, Eva Hansen, Jeff Hickman, Jim Huntley, Mike Schauer, Linda Schloegel, Greg Wallace, Nik Wogstad
Studio Manager: Cathleen Shannon
Assistant Studio Manager: Rena Tassone
Lead Photographer: Mike Parker
Photographers: Rex Irmen, John Lauenstein, Bill Lindner, Mark Macemon, Paul Najlis, Mette Nielsen
Contributing Photographers: Phil Aarestad, Charles Nields
Food Stylist: Nancy J. Johnson
Contributing Food Stylists: Sherri Biss, Sue Brue, Mari Lou Callahan, Anna Dimants, Beth Emmons, Brenda Fitterer, Darcy Gorris, Carol Grones, Melinda Hutchison, Marilyn Krome, Abigail Leech, Valerie Sayre, Cindy Syme
Printed on American paper by: R. R. Donnelley & Sons (0992)

CY DE COSSE INCORPORATED
Chairman: Cy DeCosse
President: James B. Maus
Executive Vice President: William B. Jones

Library of Congress Cataloging-in-Publication Data

Methven, Barbara.
  100 ideas for today's chicken / by Barbara Methven.

  p.   cm. — (Microwave cooking library)
Includes index.
ISBN 0-86573-574-3

  1. Cookery (Chicken) 2. Microwave cookery. I. Title. II. Title: One hundred ideas for today's chicken. III. Series.
TX750.5.C45M48   1992
641.6'65 — dc20   92-11260

Additional volumes in the Microwave Cooking Library series are available from the publisher:

• Basic Microwaving
• Recipe Conversion for Microwave
• Microwaving Meats
• Microwave Baking & Desserts
• Microwaving Meals in 30 Minutes
• Microwaving on a Diet
• Microwaving Fruits & Vegetables
• Microwaving Convenience Foods

• Microwaving for Holidays & Parties
• Microwaving for One & Two
• The Microwave & Freezer
• 101 Microwaving Secrets
• Microwaving Light & Healthy
• Microwaving Poultry & Seafood
• Microwaving America's Favorites
• Microwaving Fast & Easy Main Dishes

• More Microwaving Secrets
• Microwaving Light Meals & Snacks
• Holiday Microwave Ideas
• Easy Microwave Menus
• Low-fat Microwave Meals
• Cool Quick Summer Microwaving
• Ground Beef Microwave Meals
• Microwave Speed Meals

• One Pound of Imagination: Main Dishes
• One-dish Meals
• Light Meals with Meat

Contents

Finger Foods & Mini Meals

Satisfying Salads

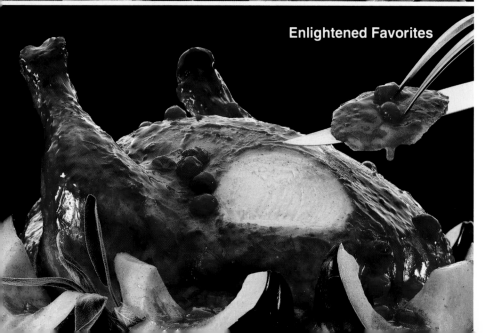

Enlightened Favorites

Before You Start

Culinary fashions change, but the popularity of chicken never wanes. Cooks prize chicken for its versatility, flavor and reasonable cost. Chicken's low fat content makes it an ideal choice for today's light, healthy meals.

To satisfy consumer preferences and for convenience, markets package chicken in a variety of forms. You can buy chicken whole, cut up or quartered. You can also select only breasts if you prefer white meat, or choose thighs for earthy dishes with robust sauces. If chicken is finger food in your family, satisfy everyone by buying enough drumsticks or wings for all. Another convenience is boneless skinless chicken. It is waste-free, cooks quickly and evenly, and eliminates preparing chicken for stir-fries or fajitas.

How to Use This Book

In *100 Ideas for Today's Chicken*, quick-idea pages introduce each section. A basic recipe provides a simple preparation technique that can be used in a variety of ways. The ideas that follow are more than variations; each produces a distinctive dish that is fast and easy to prepare. Recipes and additional quick ideas conclude each section.

> Look for Idea Boxes throughout each recipe section.

Finger Foods & Mini Meals. Use the recipes in this section as appetizers, satisfying snacks or a substantial meal for one or two.

Satisfying Salads. A wide range of recipes and quick ideas combines chicken with greens, pasta, rice, bulgur or fruit in imaginative salads to serve warm or chilled.

Enlightened Favorites. We've updated traditional family pleasers to lower fat and calorie content but keep the flavor you love. When chicken is cooked with skin on, the nutritional information for the recipe includes the fat, calories and cholesterol of the skin. Removing skin before serving reduces these values significantly.

Skillet Meals. This section features a quick-idea stir-fry to use four ways, and six seasoning mixes. Each mix can be used to make three to six different skillet meals.

Meals for One & Two

Meals for One & Two. The quick ideas for single servings use convenient prepared boneless chicken breast fillets. Other recipes in the section call for chicken parts. If you can't buy parts in quantities small enough for one or two servings, set aside the amount you need and freeze the remainder immediately.

Skinny Chicken. Chicken is naturally low in fat and calories, and these main-dish recipes make it more so. Most are under 350 calories per serving; many are even lower. Recipes are kept low in fat, salt and calories by using products like low-sodium chicken broth, lean sour cream or evaporated skim milk.

Nutritional Information

Per serving nutritional values and exchanges for weight loss follow each recipe. When a recipe serves four to six persons, the analysis applies to the greater number of servings. In the case of alternate ingredients, the analysis applies to the first ingredient listed. Optional ingredients are not included in the analysis.

Skinny Chicken

Buying & Storing Chicken

The *broiler-fryer* is by far the most popular class of chicken. When a recipe calls for "chicken," it generally means one of these young birds, which weigh 2½ to 4½ pounds when whole. Although they are most frequently sold cut up, whole broiler-fryers are available. Any cooking method suits the tender broiler-fryer, including roasting.

Roasters are sold only as whole birds. They are marketed at 8 to 12 weeks of age and weigh a little more than broiler-fryers, ranging from 4¾ to 7½ pounds.

Capons, sold whole for roasting, are neutered male chickens weighing from 6 to 9 pounds.

Stewing hens are mature female chickens, weighing from 4 to 6 pounds. Although flavorful, they require long, slow cooking to tenderize and are unsuitable for microwaving.

When you buy chicken parts, you are buying broiler-fryers. Boneless chicken parts cost more per pound than bone-in, but the difference in price appears greater than it really is (see photo right).

When you buy whole or cut-up chicken, remember that greater weight means more meat, not more bone. A 2½-pound bird serves four, while a 3½-pound bird serves six.

How to Store Chicken

Many supermarkets date chicken packages. In some, this is the date on which they package the chicken; in others, it is a "sell by" date. If you are not sure, ask the meat cutter. Vacuum-packed seasoned boneless chicken breast fillets have a "use by" date stamped on them by the processor.

With the exception of these vacuum-packed fillets, chicken should be used within two days of purchase. If you plan to keep it longer than that, freeze it.

Like any food that must be kept cold to prevent bacterial growth, chicken should be among the last items you put in your shopping cart before heading for the check-out counter. Take it home directly and store promptly in the refrigerator. Place the chicken package in an additional plastic bag or on a plate to catch any dripping juices, which could carry bacteria to other foods.

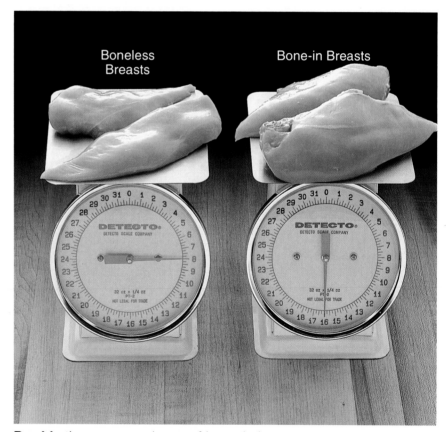

Double the per pound cost of bone-in breasts to compare their price with boneless meat. While ½ pound of boneless chicken breast serves two, you need 1 pound of bone-in breast to get the same amount of meat.

How to Cook Chicken

Bone-in. Meat near bone is no longer pink and juices run clear.

Most of a chicken's fat is in, or just under, the skin, so skinless chicken contains about half the fat of skin-on chicken. Studies show that, as long as you skin chicken before eating it, leaving skin on during cooking does not affect fat content of the meat appreciably.

During roasting and grilling, the skin helps hold in juices. Chicken that is cooked in a sauce should be skinned before cooking so the meat, not the skin, absorbs the flavors and fat does not melt into the sauce.

For safety, cook chicken thoroughly; for flavor and juiciness, don't overcook it. Be especially careful when cooking skinless chicken pieces by conventional methods. Microwaving is less likely to dry out skinless chicken, so overcooking should not be a problem.

To kill harmful bacteria, cook whole chickens until internal temperature in thickest portions of both thighs registers 185°F, meat near bone is no longer pink and juices run clear. A whole chicken breast will be done at 170°F. Check internal temperature with an instant-read thermometer. Use the visual test (right) for smaller pieces of chicken.

Boneless. Meat is no longer pink and juices run clear.

Never leave cooked chicken at room temperature for more than 1 hour. Serve hot foods hot and cold foods well chilled. Refrigerate leftovers promptly. To speed cooling, divide large amounts into small, shallow containers.

Food Safety Tips

Follow standard food safety practices, such as washing hands, utensils and cutting boards with hot, soapy water before and after contact with uncooked poultry. Use paper towels for cleanup, and discard immediately.

Don't let raw chicken juices come in contact with other foods.

Unwrap and handle chicken on a plastic cutting board. Cracks in a wooden board can harbor bacteria, even after washing.

Always marinate chicken in the refrigerator, not at room temperature.

If marinade is to be used as a sauce, reserve some for this purpose and add chicken to the remainder. Do not reuse marinade.

Don't place cooked chicken or other foods on a plate that has been used to hold raw poultry. When grilling, use separate plates for carrying raw and cooked meat, or line your platter with plastic wrap to carry raw chicken. When food is on the grill, discard plastic wrap, leaving a clean platter for cooked meat.

Choosing Today's Chicken

Today's convenient chicken comes cut in many ways and packaged in quantities from "family size" to under a pound. In some cases, preparations such as boning and skinning are done for you. This chart pictures some of the most popular forms of chicken offered in today's meat cases. Use it to help you identify a variety of cuts.

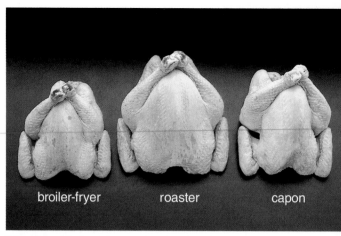

Whole chickens may be broiler-fryers, roasters, capons or hens, depending upon age and weight. Larger birds usually include a giblet pack (neck, heart, liver and gizzard); remove before cooking.

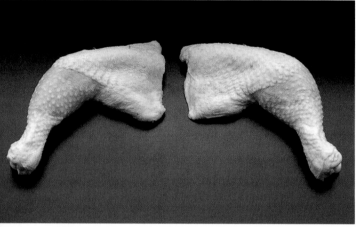

Whole broiler legs are the thigh-drumstick combination without back portion.

Broiler thighs are the upper portion of the leg quarter and are cut with or without backbone. They are also available as boneless skinless thighs.

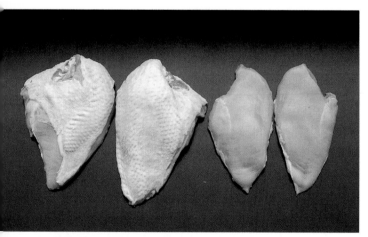

Broiler split breasts are breast quarters with wings removed. They may include a portion of the back. Boneless split breasts are marketed with or without skin.

Chicken wings are marketed whole or in portions that include the **drumette**, or first section of the wing, and the **midsection**, or flat center piece, sold with or without the tip.

Whole cut-up chickens are broiler-fryers cut into 2 breast halves with ribs and back portion, 2 thighs with back portion, 2 drumsticks and 2 wings.

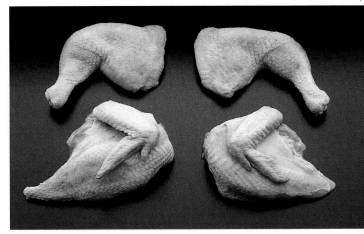

Whole quartered chickens are broiler-fryers cut into 2 leg quarters, including thigh, drumstick and part of the back, and 2 breast quarters with wings and backbone attached.

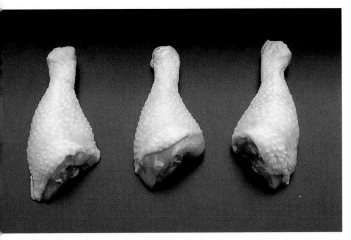

Broiler drumsticks are the lower portion of the leg. To skin them before cooking, snip the skin lengthwise with a kitchen shears and remove.

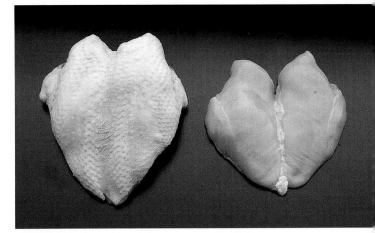

Whole broiler breasts are marketed skin on or skinless, with or without bone.

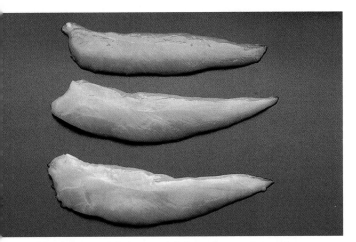

Boneless skinless chicken breast tenders are the tenderloin portions of boneless breasts.

Ground chicken varies in fat content. The product used in this book was 90% fat free, and a combination of dark and white meat.

Finger Foods & Mini Meals

Sante Fe Drumettes
Chicken & Spinach Phyllo Bundles
Zesty Pineapple Chicken & Shrimp Kabobs
Cocktail Chicken Meatballs

Chicken Lite Bites

¾ lb. boneless skinless chicken breast tenders (12 tenders)

Stuffers:
Canned whole water chestnuts
Pineapple chunks
Pimiento-stuffed green olives
Pitted black olives, stuffed with carrot strips
Marinated artichoke hearts
Pickled Tuscan peppers
Green onion brushes
Green and red pepper chunks
Canned baby corn on the cob

Instant Marinades & Dips:
Italian dressing
Catalina or French dressing
Teriyaki sauce
Vinaigrette
Sweet-and-sour sauce

12 servings

Wrap tenders around one or more of above stuffers. Secure with wooden picks. Place in shallow dish. Pour ¼ to ½ cup of desired marinade over chicken bites. Let stand for 10 to 15 minutes, turning once or twice, or cover with plastic wrap and chill 1 to 2 hours. Drain and discard marinade. Arrange chicken bites on roasting rack. Cover with wax paper or microwave cooking paper. Microwave at High for 3½ to 4½ minutes, or until meat is no longer pink, rotating rack and turning chicken bites over once. Serve with desired dip.

Polynesian Skewered Snacks

¾ lb. boneless skinless chicken breast tenders
  (12 tenders)
  Strips of fully cooked deli sliced ham, cut
    length and width of chicken tenders
  Green onion brushes
  Red and green pepper chunks
  Pineapple chunks
  Red and green apple chunks

Marinade:

½ cup orange marmalade
 2 tablespoons teriyaki sauce

12 servings

On 6-inch wooden skewers, skewer tenders with one or more of remaining ingredients. Arrange skewers in shallow baking dish. Set aside. In 2-cup measure, combine marinade ingredients. Microwave at High for 1 to 1½ minutes, or until mixture is hot and can be stirred smooth, stirring once. Cool slightly. Pour evenly over skewers. Let stand for 10 to 15 minutes, turning once or twice, or cover with plastic wrap and chill 1 to 2 hours. Drain and discard marinade. Arrange skewers on roasting rack. Cover with wax paper or microwave cooking paper. Microwave at High for 6 to 8 minutes, or until meat is no longer pink, rotating rack and turning skewers over once. Sprinkle with toasted coconut, if desired.

14

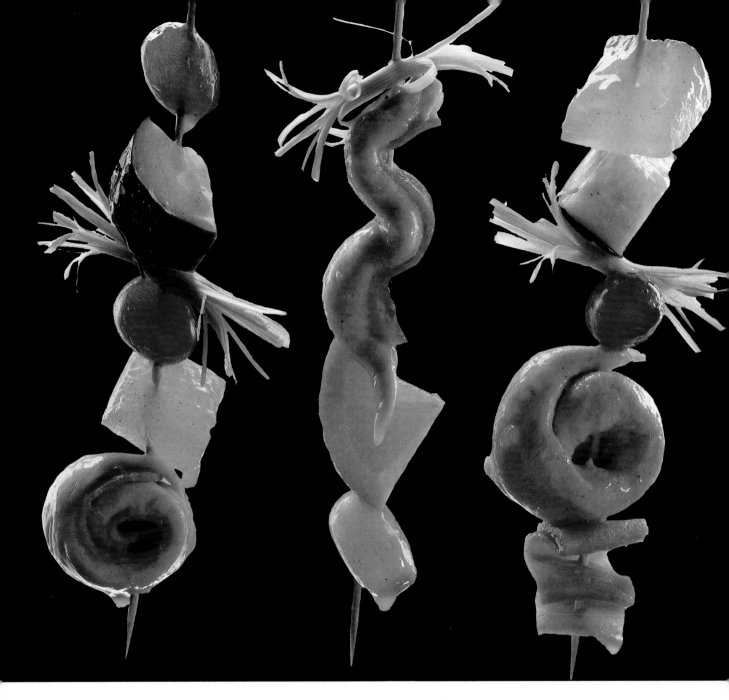

Curried Chicken Snack Sticks

¾ lb. boneless skinless chicken breast tenders
    (12 tenders)
    Watermelon pickle chunks
    Red and green seedless grapes
    Cucumber chunks
    Orange wedges
    Strips of fully cooked deli sliced ham, cut
    length and width of chicken tenders
    Green onion brushes

Marinade:
½ cup peach preserves
 1 tablespoon vegetable oil
 1 teaspoon curry powder

On 6-inch wooden skewers, skewer tenders and one or more of remaining ingredients. Arrange skewers in shallow baking dish. Set aside. In 2-cup measure, combine marinade ingredients. Microwave at High for 1 to 1½ minutes, or until mixture is hot and can be stirred smooth, stirring once. Cool slightly. Pour evenly over skewers. Let stand for 10 to 15 minutes, turning once or twice, or cover with plastic wrap and chill 1 to 2 hours. Drain and discard marinade. Arrange skewers on roasting rack. Cover with wax paper or microwave cooking paper. Microwave at High for 6 to 8 minutes, or until meat is no longer pink, rotating rack and turning skewers over once.

12 servings

Miniature Egg Rolls

½ lb. ground chicken, crumbled
¼ cup sliced green onions
3 tablespoons shredded carrot
2 tablespoons plum sauce
2 tablespoons finely chopped water chestnuts
2 teaspoons soy sauce
1 teaspoon sherry
¼ teaspoon five-spice powder
¼ teaspoon garlic powder
⅛ teaspoon ground ginger
1 egg yolk, beaten with 2 teaspoons water
18 wonton skins (3½-inch square)

6 servings

In 2-quart casserole, combine chicken and onions. Microwave at High for 2½ to 4 minutes, or until meat is no longer pink, stirring once to break apart. Drain. Add remaining ingredients, except egg yolk mixture and wonton skins. Mix well. Spoon 1 tablespoon chicken mixture just below center of each wonton skin. Roll up, folding in sides. Brush top corners with egg yolk mixture; continue rolling to complete seal.

In deep 10-inch skillet, heat ¼ inch vegetable oil conventionally over medium-high heat. Fry egg rolls, 5 at a time, for 2 to 3 minutes, or until golden brown, turning 2 or 3 times. Drain on paper-towel-lined plate. Serve egg rolls with additional plum sauce for dipping.

Per Serving: Calories: 202 • Protein: 10 g.
• Carbohydrate: 15 g. • Fat: 11 g.
• Cholesterol: 67 mg. • Sodium: 165 mg.
Exchanges: ¾ starch, ¾ lean meat, ¾ vegetable, 1¾ fat

Chicken Little Tacos

- 1 boneless whole chicken breast (8 to 10 oz.), split in half, skin removed
- ½ cup tomato sauce
- ¼ cup water
- 1 teaspoon chili powder
- ¼ teaspoon ground cumin
- ¼ teaspoon dried oregano leaves
- ¼ teaspoon garlic powder
- ¼ teaspoon onion powder
- 24 miniature taco shells
- ½ cup finely shredded leaf lettuce
- ½ cup finely chopped seeded tomato
- ½ cup finely shredded Cheddar cheese

12 servings

Place chicken in 8-inch square baking dish. Cover with wax paper or microwave cooking paper. Microwave at High for 4 to 6 minutes, or until meat is no longer pink and juices run clear, rearranging once. Drain. Cool slightly. Shred into small pieces.

In 10-inch nonstick skillet, combine chicken, tomato sauce, water, chili powder, cumin, oregano, garlic powder and onion powder. Cook conventionally over medium heat for 6 to 10 minutes, or until mixture thickens, stirring frequently. Set aside.

Arrange taco shells on serving plate. Microwave at High for 1 to 1½ minutes, or until warm, rotating plate once. Fill each taco shell with 1 tablespoon seasoned chicken mixture. Top each taco evenly with lettuce, tomato and cheese.

Per Serving: Calories: 95 • Protein: 6 g.
• Carbohydrate: 6 g. • Fat: 5 g.
• Cholesterol: 17 mg. • Sodium: 144 mg.
Exchanges: ⅓ starch, ½ lean meat,
⅓ vegetable, ¾ fat

Mexicana Bite-size Pies ◀

1 pkg. (15 oz.) refrigerated
   prepared pie crusts

Filling:

1 cup cut-up cooked chicken
1 cup shredded Monterey
   Jack cheese
1 can (4 oz.) chopped green
   chilies, drained
1/3 cup sliced black olives
1/3 cup sliced green onions
1 teaspoon chili powder
1/2 teaspoon onion salt
3 eggs
1 cup milk

Garnish:

   Sliced black olives
   Sliced green onions

9 servings

Per Serving: Calories: 339 • Protein: 12 g.
• Carbohydrate: 24 g. • Fat: 21 g.
• Cholesterol: 113 mg. • Sodium: 516 mg.
Exchanges: 1 1/4 starch, 1 lean meat,
1/4 vegetable, 1/4 skim milk, 3 1/2 fat

Artichoke & Chicken ◀
Bite-size Pies

1 pkg. (15 oz.) refrigerated
   prepared pie crusts

Filling:

1 cup cut-up cooked chicken
1 jar (6.5 oz.) marinated
   artichoke hearts, drained
   and chopped
1/3 cup grated Parmesan
   cheese
1/4 cup sliced green onions
1/4 cup mayonnaise
1/2 teaspoon dry mustard
1/4 teaspoon onion salt
3 eggs
1 cup milk

Garnish:

   Chopped seeded tomato
   Snipped fresh chives

9 servings

Per Serving: Calories: 362 • Protein: 11 g.
• Carbohydrate: 25 g. • Fat: 24 g.
• Cholesterol: 108 mg. • Sodium: 486 mg.
Exchanges: 1 1/4 starch, 1 lean meat,
1/2 vegetable, 1/4 skim milk, 4 fat

How to Make Bite-size Pies

Cut nine 3-inch circles from each
pie crust. Press circles into bottom and up sides of eighteen
2 3/4 × 2-inch muffin cups.

Heat conventional oven to
400°F. Chill crust-lined muffin
cups 30 minutes.

In medium mixing bowl, combine filling ingredients. Microwave filling at High for 3 1/2 to 5
minutes, or until mixture is hot
and just begins to set around
edges, stirring twice.

Spoon about 3 tablespoons filling into each crust-lined cup.
Bake conventionally for 20 to
25 minutes, or until pies are
puffed and golden brown and
knife inserted in center comes
out clean. Let stand for 10 minutes. Loosen and remove pies
from pan. Sprinkle with garnish.

Herb & Mushroom Mini Calzones

1 boneless whole chicken breast (8 to 10 oz.), split in half, skin removed
½ teaspoon onion powder

Filling:

½ cup grated Parmesan cheese
1 jar (2.5 oz.) sliced mushrooms, drained
¼ cup mayonnaise
¼ cup sour cream
¼ cup sliced green onions
½ teaspoon dried dill weed

1 pkg. (15 oz.) refrigerated prepared pie crusts
1 egg, beaten with 1 teaspoon water

6 to 8 servings

Per Serving: Calories: 379 • Protein: 13 g.
• Carbohydrate: 25 g. • Fat: 25 g.
• Cholesterol: 73 mg. • Sodium: 413 mg.
Exchanges: 1½ starch, 1 lean meat, ½ vegetable, 4¼ fat

Curried Chicken Mini Calzones ▶

1 boneless whole chicken breast (8 to 10 oz.), split in half, skin removed
½ teaspoon onion powder

Filling:

½ cup frozen chopped broccoli, defrosted and well drained
⅓ cup chopped pecans
¼ cup mayonnaise
¼ cup sour cream
1 teaspoon lemon juice
½ to 1 teaspoon curry powder

1 pkg. (15 oz.) refrigerated prepared pie crusts
1 egg, beaten with 1 teaspoon water

6 to 8 servings

Per Serving: Calories: 377 • Protein: 10 g.
• Carbohydrate: 26 g. • Fat: 26 g.
• Cholesterol: 66 mg. • Sodium: 278 mg.
Exchanges: 1½ starch, ½ lean meat, ¾ vegetable, 4¾ fat

How to Make Mini Calzones

Place chicken in 8-inch square baking dish. Sprinkle evenly with onion powder. Cover with wax paper or microwave cooking paper. Microwave at High for 4 to 6 minutes, or until meat is no longer pink and juices run clear, rearranging once. Drain. Cool completely. Cut chicken into ¼-inch cubes. Heat conventional oven to 375°F. In medium mixing bowl, combine chicken and filling ingredients. Cut seven 4-inch circles from each pie crust, reusing trimmings. Place heaping tablespoon filling on half of each circle, ¼ inch from edge.

Fold other half over. Press edges with fork to seal. Place calzones on large baking sheet. Bake for 20 to 25 minutes, or until golden brown, brushing with beaten egg mixture during last 5 minutes of baking time.

Bite-size Burger Buns

4 pieces frozen unbaked
   dinner roll dough
1 egg yolk, beaten with
   2 teaspoons water
   Poppy, caraway or sesame
   seed

8 servings

Per Serving: Calories: 58 • Protein: 2 g.
• Carbohydrate: 8 g. • Fat: 2 g.
• Cholesterol: 27 mg. • Sodium: 1 mg.
Exchanges: ½ starch, ½ fat

How to Make Bite-size Burger Buns

Spray 9-inch pie plate with non-stick vegetable cooking spray. Place frozen dough in pie plate. Cover with wax paper or microwave cooking paper.

Microwave at 30% (Medium Low) for 1 to 2 minutes, or just until dough is warm to the touch, rotating plate every 30 seconds. Cut each roll in half.

Spray large baking sheet with nonstick vegetable cooking spray. Place roll halves cut-side-down on prepared baking sheet. Pat lightly to shape. Tear off large sheet of plastic wrap.

Spray 1 side with nonstick vegetable cooking spray. Cover rolls loosely with plastic wrap, sprayed-side-down. Let stand in warm place for 45 minutes to 1 hour, or until doubled in size.

Heat conventional oven to 350°F. Brush tops of rolls with egg yolk mixture. Sprinkle with poppy seed. Bake for 15 to 20 minutes, or until light golden brown. Cool on cooling rack. Split buns in half crosswise.

Midwest Barbecue

California Ranch

Bite-size Burgers

1 lb. ground chicken, crumbled
¼ cup unseasoned dry bread crumbs
¼ cup sliced green onions
1 egg, beaten
2 tablespoons grated Parmesan cheese
2 teaspoons snipped fresh parsley
½ teaspoon dry mustard
¼ teaspoon salt
⅛ teaspoon pepper

8 servings

In medium mixing bowl, combine all ingredients. Shape mixture into eight 2-inch patties. Arrange patties on roasting rack. Cover with wax paper or microwave cooking paper. Microwave at High for 5 to 6½ minutes, or until burgers are firm and no longer pink, rearranging once. Serve burgers in buns (opposite). Garnish with lettuce, tomato, onion and pickle slices, if desired.

Per Serving: Calories: 174 • Protein: 14 g. • Carbohydrate: 11 g.
• Fat: 8 g. • Cholesterol: 101 mg. • Sodium: 169 mg.
Exchanges: ¾ starch, 1⅔ lean meat, ½ fat

Idea: **Midwest Barbecue Burgers:** Prepare as directed left, except substitute barbecue sauce for Parmesan cheese.

Idea: **California Ranch:** Prepare as directed left, except substitute 2 teaspoons ranch dressing mix for Parmesan cheese. Omit dry mustard. Serve topped with prepared ranch dressing, if desired.

Idea: **Mexican Hot! Burgers:** Prepare as directed left, except substitute chopped canned jalapeño peppers for Parmesan cheese, 1 teaspoon chili powder for snipped fresh parsley and ground cumin for dry mustard.

Idea: **Italian Herb Burgers:** Prepare as directed left, except substitute Italian seasoned bread crumbs for unseasoned bread crumbs and Italian seasoning for dry mustard.

Italian Herb

Mexican Hot!

Bite-size Burger

◀ Barbecued Pita Sandwiches

 2 boneless whole chicken breasts (8 to 10 oz. each), split in half, skin removed, cut into 1 to 2-inch strips
 ¼ cup chopped onion
 2 cloves garlic, minced
1½ teaspoons seasoned salt
 ½ teaspoon chili powder
 1 cup thinly sliced green pepper
 1 cup barbecue sauce
 ¼ cup water
  Shredded lettuce
 4 pita loaves (6-inch), cut into quarters

8 servings

In 2-quart casserole, combine chicken, onion, garlic, seasoned salt and chili powder. Microwave at High for 4 to 9 minutes, or until meat is no longer pink, stirring twice. Drain.

Add green pepper, barbecue sauce and water. Mix well. Microwave at 70% (Medium High) for 12 to 15 minutes, or until mixture is hot and flavors are blended. To serve, spoon mixture evenly into lettuce-lined pita quarters.

Per Serving: Calories: 185 • Protein: 16 g. • Carbohydrate: 24 g. • Fat: 2 g. • Cholesterol: 35 mg. • Sodium: 698 mg.
Exchanges: 1 starch, 1½ lean meat, 1 vegetable, ¼ fruit

◀ Sandwich Spirals

 1 pkg. (3 oz.) cream cheese
 2 teaspoons mayonnaise
 ½ teaspoon prepared mustard
 ½ teaspoon dried chives
 1 sheet soft cracker bread (15-inch)
 6 slices (1 oz. each) fully cooked chicken
 6 slices (1 oz. each) Monterey Jack cheese
 1 cup fresh spinach leaves
 1 medium tomato, thinly sliced

6 to 8 servings

In small mixing bowl, microwave cream cheese at High for 15 to 30 seconds, or until softened. Add mayonnaise, mustard and chives. Mix well. Spread cream cheese mixture evenly over cracker bread. Layer remaining ingredients on cracker bread, leaving about 4 inches at one end covered with cream cheese mixture only.

Starting at filled end, roll up, jelly roll style, enclosing filling. Wrap with plastic wrap. Chill at least 1 hour. Slice with serrated knife.

Per Serving: Calories: 242 • Protein: 15 g. • Carbohydrate: 15 g. • Fat: 14 g. • Cholesterol: 50 mg. • Sodium: 274 mg.
Exchanges: 1 starch, 1¾ lean meat, ¼ vegetable, 1½ fat

Chicken Salad Puff Rings

Filling:

1 1/2	cups cut-up cooked chicken
1	jar (6 oz.) marinated artichoke hearts, drained and chopped
1/2	cup shredded carrot
1/4	cup mayonnaise
1/4	cup sour cream
1/4	cup sliced green onions
1/4	cup grated Parmesan cheese
1	tablespoon milk
1	cup hot water
1/2	cup margarine or butter
1 1/4	cups all-purpose flour
1/4	teaspoon salt
4	eggs

16 servings

In medium mixing bowl, combine filling ingredients. Cover with plastic wrap. Chill. Heat conventional oven to 400°F. Spray 2 large baking sheets with nonstick vegetable cooking spray. Set aside.

In 8-cup measure, combine water and margarine. Microwave at High for 3 to 5 minutes, or until margarine is melted. Add flour and salt. Stir vigorously until mixture forms a ball. Add 1 egg at a time, beating after each addition.

Drop 8 scant 1/4-cup dollops of dough in circle on each prepared baking sheet, with dollops touching. Bake conventionally for 25 to 30 minutes, or until rings are puffed and golden brown. Cool for 20 minutes.

Remove rings from baking sheets. Carefully cut each in half crosswise. Spoon half of filling mixture evenly into bottom half of each puff ring. Add tops. Serve immediately.

Per Serving: Calories: 182 • Protein: 7 g.
• Carbohydrate: 9 g. • Fat: 13 g.
• Cholesterol: 70 mg. • Sodium: 229 mg.
Exchanges: 1/2 starch, 3/4 lean meat,
1/4 vegetable, 2 fat

Easy Chili Nacho Bites

4 flour tortillas (8-inch)
1 lb. ground chicken, crumbled
½ teaspoon onion powder
½ teaspoon ground cumin
½ teaspoon chili powder
¼ teaspoon garlic powder
1 pkg. (3 oz.) cream cheese
½ cup shredded Cheddar cheese
¼ cup canned chopped green chilies, drained

8 servings

Heat conventional oven to 375°F. Cut tortillas into quarters. Place on large baking sheet. Bake for 8 to 10 minutes, or until lightly browned and crisp. Set aside.

In 2-quart casserole, combine chicken, onion powder, cumin, chili powder and garlic powder. Microwave at High for 4 to 6 minutes, or until meat is no longer pink, stirring once or twice to break apart. Drain. Set aside.

In small mixing bowl, microwave cream cheese at High for 15 to 30 seconds, or until softened. Add Cheddar cheese and green chilies. Mix well. Spoon scant 1 tablespoon cream cheese mixture onto each tortilla quarter. Top each with small amount of chicken mixture. Place 4 or 5 tortilla quarters on paper-towel-lined plate.

Microwave at High for 1½ to 2 minutes, or until nachos are hot and cheese begins to melt. Repeat with remaining tortilla quarters. Garnish with salsa and fresh cilantro leaves, if desired.

Per Serving: Calories: 213 • Protein: 14 g. • Carbohydrate: 13 g. • Fat: 11 g.
• Cholesterol: 66 mg. • Sodium: 254 mg.
Exchanges: ¾ starch, 1¾ lean meat, 1¼ fat

Quesadillas with Cilantro Pesto

Pesto:

½ cup snipped fresh cilantro
    leaves
¼ cup sour cream
¼ cup mayonnaise
1 teaspoon lemon juice
¼ teaspoon hot pepper sauce

½ teaspoon chili powder
¼ teaspoon ground cumin
⅛ teaspoon dried oregano
    leaves
1 boneless whole chicken
    breast (8 to 10 oz.), split in
    half, skin removed
8 flour tortillas (8-inch)
1 cup refried beans
1 cup shredded Cheddar
    cheese
1 cup shredded Monterey
    Jack cheese
¼ cup canned chopped
    green chilies, drained

8 servings

In small mixing bowl, combine pesto ingredients. Cover with plastic wrap. Chill. In small bowl, combine chili powder, cumin and oregano. Place chicken in 8-inch square baking dish. Sprinkle both sides of chicken evenly with chili powder mixture. Cover with wax paper or microwave cooking paper. Microwave at High for 4 to 6 minutes, or until meat is no longer pink and juices run clear, rearranging once. Drain. Cool slightly.

Shred chicken into small pieces. Spread each of 4 tortillas evenly with refried beans. Sprinkle each evenly with chicken mixture, Cheddar cheese, Monterey Jack cheese and chilies. Top with remaining tortillas.

Spray 10-inch nonstick skillet with nonstick vegetable cooking spray. Heat conventionally over medium heat. Carefully place 1 filled tortilla in skillet. Cook for 8 to 10 minutes, or until light golden brown, turning once. Repeat with remaining tortillas. Cut each quesadilla into quarters. Serve with pesto and top with salsa, if desired.

Per Serving: Calories: 366 • Protein: 19 g. • Carbohydrate: 31 g. • Fat: 18 g.
• Cholesterol: 52 mg. • Sodium: 597 mg.
Exchanges: 1¾ starch, 1¾ lean meat, 1 vegetable, 2½ fat

Tex-Mex Barbecue Pie ▲

½ lb. ground chicken, crumbled
½ cup chopped green pepper
¼ cup chopped onion
1 can (16 oz.) pinto beans, rinsed and drained
⅓ cup barbecue sauce
½ teaspoon seasoned salt

¼ teaspoon chili powder
1 pkg. (15 oz.) refrigerated prepared pie crusts
⅓ cup shredded Cheddar cheese
Paprika

10 to 12 servings

Heat conventional oven to 375°F. In 2-quart casserole, combine chicken, green pepper and onion. Microwave at High for 3½ to 5 minutes, or until meat is no longer pink, stirring once or twice to break apart. Drain. Add beans, barbecue sauce, seasoned salt and chili powder. Mix well.

Unfold 1 pie crust and place on 12-inch pizza pan or large baking sheet. Spoon meat mixture onto dough to within ¾ inch of edge of crust. Sprinkle evenly with cheese. Unfold remaining pie crust. Cut slits in top crust to vent, or use decorative cookie cutter to cut shape from center of crust. Place pie crust over filling. Roll up edges; flute or press with fork to seal. Sprinkle lightly with paprika. Bake conventionally for 35 to 37 minutes, or until crust is golden brown. Serve in wedges.

Per Serving: Calories: 228 • Protein: 7 g. • Carbohydrate: 21 g. • Fat: 13 g.
• Cholesterol: 29 mg. • Sodium: 343 mg.
Exchanges: 1¼ starch, ½ lean meat, ½ vegetable, 2¼ fat

Idea: **Chicken Pizza Pie:**
Prepare as directed left, except increase ground chicken to 1 lb. and green pepper to 1 cup. Microwave chicken mixture as directed, except increase cooking time to 4 to 6 minutes. Omit beans. Substitute pizza sauce for barbecue sauce, Italian seasoning for seasoned salt, and garlic powder for chili powder. Omit paprika. Substitute 1 cup shredded mozzarella cheese for Cheddar cheese.

Three-pepper Chicken & Artichoke Pizza

- 1 tablespoon yellow cornmeal
- 1 pkg. (10 oz.) refrigerated pizza crust dough
- 1/3 cup grated Parmesan cheese
- 3/4 cup each green, red, and yellow pepper strips
- 1/4 cup sliced green onions
- 2 tablespoons snipped fresh basil leaves
- 1 tablespoon margarine or butter
- 2 cloves garlic, minced
- 2 cups shredded mozzarella cheese, divided
- 1 jar (6 oz.) marinated artichoke hearts, drained and chopped
- 1/2 cup sliced black olives
- 1 cup cut-up cooked chicken

8 servings

Heat conventional oven to 400°F. Grease 15½ × 10½ × 1-inch jelly roll pan. Sprinkle evenly with cornmeal. Press crust into bottom and up sides of prepared pan. Bake for 8 to 10 minutes, or until light golden brown. Sprinkle crust evenly with Parmesan cheese. Set aside.

In 2-quart casserole, place peppers, onions, basil, margarine and garlic. Microwave at High for 3 to 4 minutes, or until peppers are tender, stirring once. Drain. Sprinkle 3/4 cup mozzarella cheese over crust. Spoon pepper mixture evenly over crust. Top with artichokes, olives and chicken. Sprinkle remaining 1¼ cups mozzarella evenly over pizza. Bake conventionally for 14 to 18 minutes, or until cheese is melted and crust is golden brown. Serve in squares.

Per Serving: Calories: 279 • Protein: 16 g. • Carbohydrate: 22 g. • Fat: 14 g. • Cholesterol: 40 mg. • Sodium: 553 mg.
Exchanges: 1¼ starch, 1½ lean meat, 3/4 vegetable, 2 fat

Idea: Chicken Sausage Pizza: Prepare as directed above, except substitute chicken sausage (below) for cut-up cooked chicken.

Chicken Sausage: In small mixing bowl, combine 1/2 lb. ground chicken, 1/2 teaspoon fennel seed, 1/4 teaspoon crushed red pepper flakes and 1/4 teaspoon garlic powder. Drop mixture by heaping teaspoons into 10-inch square casserole. Microwave at High for 2½ to 4 minutes, or until sausage is firm and no longer pink, stirring to rearrange once or twice. Drain.

Chicken Sausage Pizza

Three-pepper Chicken & Artichoke Pizza

Hot Chili Chicken Dip

Hot Chicken & Curry
Cracker Spread

Hot Chicken & Curry Cracker Spread

1 boneless whole chicken breast (8 to 10 oz.), split in half, skin removed
1/3 cup finely chopped celery
1/4 cup finely chopped green pepper
1/4 cup finely chopped red pepper
1 tablespoon margarine or butter
1/4 cup plus 1 tablespoon sliced almonds, toasted, divided
1/2 cup mayonnaise
1/4 cup sour cream
1/4 cup grated Parmesan cheese
2 tablespoons milk
2 teaspoons lemon juice
3/4 teaspoon curry powder
1/4 teaspoon onion salt

16 servings

Place chicken in 8-inch square baking dish. Cover with wax paper or microwave cooking paper. Microwave at High for 4 to 6 minutes, or until meat is no longer pink and juices run clear, rearranging once. Drain. Cool slightly. Shred into small pieces. Set aside.

In 2-quart casserole, combine celery, peppers and margarine. Cover. Microwave at High for 2 to 3 minutes, or until vegetables are tender-crisp, stirring once. Add chicken, 1/4 cup almonds and remaining ingredients. Mix well. Cover with wax paper or microwave cooking paper. Microwave at High for 1 to 2 minutes, or until mixture is hot, stirring once. Garnish with remaining 1 tablespoon almonds. Serve with crackers.

Per Serving: Calories: 100 • Protein: 4 g.
• Carbohydrate: 1 g. • Fat: 9 g.
• Cholesterol: 16 mg. • Sodium: 109 mg.
Exchanges: 1/2 lean meat, 1 1/2 fat

Hot Chili Chicken Dip

1 tablespoon all-purpose flour
2 tablespoons milk
2 jars (4 oz. each) pasteurized process cheese spread
1 cup cut-up cooked chicken
1 can (4 oz.) chopped green chilies, drained
1/3 cup sliced black olives
1/3 cup chopped seeded tomato
1/4 teaspoon ground cumin
1/4 teaspoon cayenne

16 servings

Place flour in 1-quart casserole. Blend in milk, stirring until mixture is smooth. Add cheese spread. Microwave at High for 1 to 2 minutes, or until mixture is hot and can be stirred smooth, stirring once.

Add remaining ingredients. Mix well. Microwave at High for 5 to 6 minutes, or until mixture thickens and bubbles, stirring twice. Serve hot dip with corn chips or tortilla chips, if desired.

Per Serving: Calories: 65 • Protein: 5 g. • Carbohydrate: 2 g. • Fat: 4 g.
• Cholesterol: 18 mg. • Sodium: 311 mg.
Exchanges: 3/4 lean meat, 1/2 fat

Chicken Appetizer Terrine

5 thin red pepper strips
12 oz. cream cheese, divided
1/4 cup sliced green onions
2 teaspoons chili powder
1 1/2 cups shredded Co-Jack cheese, divided
1 cup cut-up cooked chicken
1 can (4 oz.) chopped green chilies, drained
2 tablespoons salsa
1/2 teaspoon ground cumin
1 pkg. (6 oz.) frozen guacamole
1/4 cup chopped red pepper

20 servings

Line 8 × 4-inch loaf dish with plastic wrap. Arrange red pepper strips in bottom of dish. Set aside. In medium mixing bowl, microwave 8 oz. cream cheese at 50% (Medium) for 2 1/2 to 3 1/2 minutes, or until softened. Add onions and chili powder. Mix well. Spread cheese mixture evenly in bottom of prepared loaf dish. Sprinkle with 3/4 cup Co-Jack cheese. Set aside.

In small mixing bowl, combine chicken, green chilies, salsa and cumin. Spoon mixture evenly over Co-Jack cheese layer. Set aside.

In small mixing bowl, combine guacamole and remaining 4 oz. cream cheese. Microwave at 50% (Medium) for 2 to 4 minutes, or until mixture can be stirred smooth, stirring twice. Add chopped red pepper. Mix well. Spread guacamole mixture evenly over chicken layer. Sprinkle with remaining 3/4 cup Co-Jack cheese. Cover with plastic wrap. Chill 4 hours, or until firm.

Remove plastic wrap. Invert terrine on lettuce-lined serving plate. Garnish with additional sliced green onions and chopped red pepper, if desired. Serve as spread with crackers or sliced French bread.

Per Serving: Calories: 128 • Protein: 6 g. • Carbohydrate: 2 g. • Fat: 11 g.
• Cholesterol: 33 mg. • Sodium: 208 mg.
Exchanges: 3/4 lean meat, 1/2 vegetable, 1 1/2 fat

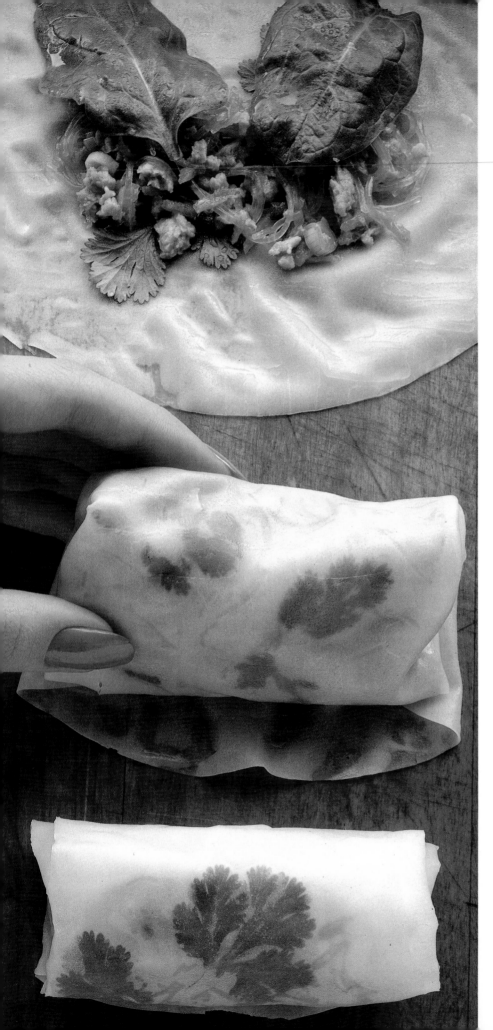

Fresh Spring Rolls

- 2 cups water
- 1 oz. uncooked cellophane noodles
- ½ lb. ground chicken, crumbled
- 2 tablespoons sliced green onion
- ½ cup shredded carrot
- 1 tablespoon soy sauce
- 1 teaspoon sesame oil
- ¼ teaspoon white pepper
- 12 round rice paper sheets (8½-inch diameter)*
- 24 sprigs fresh cilantro
- 24 whole fresh spinach leaves

12 servings

Place water in 4-cup measure. Cover with plastic wrap. Microwave at High for 4 to 6 minutes, or until water begins to boil. Place noodles in water. Re-cover. Let stand for 10 to 15 minutes, or until noodles are tender. Drain. With scissors, cut noodles into 1-inch lengths. Set aside. In 2-quart casserole, combine chicken and onion. Microwave at High for 2½ to 4 minutes, or until meat is no longer pink, stirring once to break apart. Drain. Add noodles, carrot, soy sauce, oil and pepper. Mix well. Set aside.

Wet both sides of each rice paper sheet by holding briefly under cold running water. Place wet rice paper sheets on flat work surface. Cover with dampened paper towels to prevent drying. Remove 1 sheet. Place 2 sprigs cilantro just below center. Top with 2 tablespoons meat mixture and 2 spinach leaves. Roll up, folding in sides. Repeat with remaining ingredients. Cover with plastic wrap. Chill until serving time. Serve with plum sauce, if desired.

*Rice paper sheets may be purchased in Oriental or specialty food stores. Nutritional data not available.

Per Serving: Calories: 48 • Protein: 4 g.
• Carbohydrate: 3 g. • Fat: 2 g.
• Cholesterol: 16 mg. • Sodium: 116 mg.
Exchanges: ½ lean meat, ¼ vegetable

Chicken & Spinach Phyllo Bundles

1 boneless whole chicken breast (8 to 10 oz.), split in half, skin removed
1 cup frozen cut-leaf spinach
2 tablespoons water
1/3 cup soft cheese spread with garlic and herbs
2 tablespoons margarine or butter
4 sheets frozen phyllo dough (18 × 14-inch sheets), defrosted

8 servings

Heat conventional oven to 400°F. Spray 16 miniature muffin cups with nonstick vegetable cooking spray. Set aside. Place chicken in 8-inch square baking dish. Cover with wax paper or microwave cooking paper. Microwave at High for 4 to 6 minutes, or until meat is no longer pink and juices run clear, rearranging once. Cool slightly. Cut into 1/4-inch pieces. Set aside.

In 1-quart casserole, combine spinach and water. Cover. Microwave at High for 2 to 3 minutes, or until hot, stirring once. Drain, pressing to remove excess moisture. Add cheese. Stir until cheese melts. Add chicken. Mix well. Set aside.

In small bowl, microwave margarine at High for 45 seconds to 1 minute, or until melted. Set aside. Place two 20 × 12-inch pieces of plastic wrap side by side on flat work surface. Lay first sheet of phyllo lengthwise on covered work surface. (Keep remaining sheets covered with plastic wrap.) Brush lightly with one-fourth of melted margarine. Lay second sheet of phyllo over first. Brush lightly with half of remaining margarine. Repeat with remaining 2 sheets of phyllo and remaining margarine.

With scissors, cut sheets lengthwise into quarters. Cut each strip crosswise into quarters, making 16 pieces, each approximately 4 1/2 × 3 1/2 inches. Insert each piece into prepared muffin cup, pressing phyllo to bottom and sides of cup. Fill each cup with about 1 tablespoon chicken mixture. Bake for 10 to 12 minutes, or until golden brown. Serve warm.

Per Serving: Calories: 139 • Protein: 10 g. • Carbohydrate: 9 g. • Fat: 8 g.
• Cholesterol: 30 mg. • Sodium: 158 mg.
Exchanges: 1/2 starch, 1 lean meat, 1 fat

Drumettes Italiano

Santa Fe Drumettes

Drumettes Italiano

⅓ cup Italian dressing

Coating:

½ cup grated Parmesan cheese
1 tablespoon dried parsley flakes
1 teaspoon paprika
½ teaspoon onion powder
½ teaspoon dried oregano leaves
½ teaspoon dried basil leaves

1 to 1¼ lbs. chicken wing drumettes, skin removed

3 to 4 servings

Pour Italian dressing in shallow bowl. In large plastic food-storage bag, combine coating ingredients. Dip drumettes in dressing. Add drumettes, 2 or 3 at a time, to bag. Hold bag closed. Shake to coat. Arrange drumettes on roasting rack. Microwave at High for 5 to 7 minutes, or until meat near bone is no longer pink and juices run clear, rotating rack once. Serve hot drumettes with additional Italian dressing, if desired.

Per Serving: Calories: 226 • Protein: 19 g. • Carbohydrate: 3 g. • Fat: 15 g. • Cholesterol: 47 mg. • Sodium: 395 mg. Exchanges: 2¾ lean meat, ½ vegetable, 1¼ fat

Idea: **Santa Fe Drumettes:** Prepare as directed above, except substitute ½ cup salsa for dressing and 1 package (1¼ oz.) taco seasoning mix combined with ¼ cup yellow cornmeal for coating ingredients. Serve with additional salsa, if desired.

Idea: **Greek Herb Drumettes:** Prepare as directed above, except substitute oil and vinegar dressing for Italian dressing and dried rosemary leaves for paprika. Increase oregano to 1 teaspoon. Substitute dried dill weed for basil. Serve with Cucumber Dill Dip (below).

Cucumber Dill Dip

½ cup finely chopped seeded cucumber
⅓ cup finely chopped seeded tomato
⅓ cup plain low-fat yogurt
¼ cup sour cream
1 tablespoon snipped fresh dill weed or
    1 teaspoon dried dill weed
½ teaspoon lemon juice
¼ teaspoon dried mint leaves (optional)

3 to 4 servings

In small mixing bowl, combine all ingredients. Cover with plastic wrap. Chill.

Honey Hot Legs

Marinade:

¼ cup honey
¼ cup vegetable oil
1 tablespoon sesame seed
1 tablespoon white wine
   vinegar
1 tablespoon lemon juice
1 clove garlic, minced
½ teaspoon cayenne or
   crushed red pepper flakes
½ teaspoon Chinese hot oil
   (optional)
¼ teaspoon five-spice powder

10 to 12 chicken drumsticks
   (4 oz. each), skin removed
½ teaspoon seasoned salt

        10 to 12 servings

In 2-cup measure, combine marinade ingredients. Microwave at High for 1 to 1½ minutes, or just until hot, stirring once. Cool slightly. Reserve ¼ cup marinade. Cover and chill.

Place drumsticks in large plastic food-storage bag. Pour remaining marinade over drumsticks. Secure bag. Turn to coat. Chill at least 2 hours.

Drain and discard marinade from drumsticks. In 10-inch square casserole, arrange drumsticks with thickest portions toward outside. Cover with wax paper or microwave cooking paper. Microwave at High for 15 to 20 minutes, or until drumsticks are no longer pink on exterior, rotating and rearranging once.

Arrange drumsticks on rack in broiler pan. Sprinkle evenly with seasoned salt. Brush with half of reserved marinade. Place under conventional broiler with surface of drumsticks 7 inches from heat. Broil for 3 to 5 minutes on each side, or until meat near bone is no longer pink and juices run clear, brushing frequently with remaining marinade.

Per Serving: Calories: 131 • Protein: 15 g. • Carbohydrate: 4 g. • Fat: 6 g.
• Cholesterol: 55 mg. • Sodium: 114 mg.
Exchanges: 2 lean meat, ¼ fruit

Idea: **Sweet & Spicy Barbecued Legs:** Prepare as directed above, except substitute barbecue sauce for honey.

Cocktail Chicken Meatballs

1 lb. ground chicken, crumbled
¼ cup uncooked instant mashed potato flakes
¼ cup chopped onion
1 clove garlic, minced
½ cup plus 1 teaspoon Worcestershire sauce, divided
10 slices bacon

10 servings

In medium mixing bowl, combine chicken, potato flakes, onion, garlic and 1 teaspoon Worcestershire sauce. Shape into 20 meatballs, about 1 inch in diameter. Arrange meatballs in 10-inch square casserole. Add remaining ½ cup Worcestershire sauce. Stir meatballs gently, turning to coat. Cover. Chill 30 minutes, turning over once.

Layer 3 paper towels on plate. Arrange 5 bacon slices on paper towels. Top with 3 more paper towels and remaining bacon. Cover with 1 paper towel. Microwave at High for 5 to 6 minutes, or just until bacon begins to brown and is slightly cooked.

Cut each bacon slice in half crosswise. Drain and discard Worcestershire sauce from meatballs. Wrap each meatball with 1 bacon piece. Secure with wooden pick. Arrange meatballs on roasting rack. Microwave at High for 4½ to 5½ minutes, or until meatballs are firm and no longer pink, rotating rack and rearranging meatballs once or twice. Serve hot.

Per Serving: Calories: 165 • Protein: 10 g.
• Carbohydrate: 3 g. • Fat: 12 g.
• Cholesterol: 48 mg. • Sodium: 239 mg.
Exchanges: 1½ lean meat, 1½ fat

Meatballs Olé! ▶

1 lb. ground chicken, crumbled
1 cup crushed tortilla chips
3 tablespoons taco sauce
2 tablespoons finely chopped
   onion
1 teaspoon chili powder
¼ teaspoon salt
⅛ teaspoon garlic powder

12 servings

In medium mixing bowl, combine all ingredients. Shape into 24 meatballs, about 1 inch in diameter. Arrange meatballs in 10-inch square casserole. Cover with wax paper or microwave cooking paper. Microwave at High for 6 to 8 minutes, or until meatballs are firm and no longer pink, rearranging twice. Serve with guacamole, sour cream and salsa, if desired.

Per Serving: Calories: 96 • Protein: 7 g.
• Carbohydrate: 5 g. • Fat: 5 g.
• Cholesterol: 31 mg. • Sodium: 153 mg.
Exchanges: ⅓ starch, 1 lean meat, ⅓ fat

▶ *Idea:* **Hot Mexican Meatball Hoagies:** Prepare as directed above, except spoon 3 meatballs into each of 8 split hot dog buns. Top with shredded lettuce and chopped onion and tomato. Sprinkle with shredded Cheddar cheese. Serve topped with guacamole and salsa, if desired.

Chicken & Stuffing Meatballs with Cranberry-Orange Dipping Sauce

1 lb. ground chicken, crumbled
½ cup herb-seasoned stuffing
   mix
½ to 1 teaspoon onion salt
1 egg

Sauce:

1 cup jellied cranberry sauce
2 tablespoons orange juice

12 servings

In medium mixing bowl, combine chicken, stuffing mix, onion salt and egg. Shape into 24 meatballs, about 1 inch in diameter. Arrange meatballs in 10-inch square casserole. Cover with wax paper or microwave cooking paper. Microwave at High for 6 to 8 minutes, or until meatballs are firm and no longer pink, rearranging twice. Drain. Set aside.

In small mixing bowl, combine sauce ingredients. Microwave at High for 2 to 3 minutes, or until mixture is hot and can be stirred smooth, stirring twice. Garnish sauce with orange zest, if desired. Serve meatballs with sauce.

Per Serving: Calories: 112 • Protein: 8 g. • Carbohydrate: 12 g. • Fat: 4 g.
• Cholesterol: 49 mg. • Sodium: 187 mg.
Exchanges: 1 lean meat, ⅔ fruit, ¼ fat

Chicken Strips Parmigiana ▲

¼ cup margarine or butter, divided

Crumb Coating:

⅔ cup seasoned dry bread crumbs

¼ teaspoon garlic powder

2 boneless whole chicken breasts (8 to 10 oz. each), split in half, skin removed, cut into ¾-inch strips

⅓ cup shredded mozzarella cheese

Dipping Sauce:

1 cup pizza or spaghetti sauce

8 to 10 servings

In small mixing bowl, microwave 2 tablespoons margarine at High for 45 seconds to 1 minute, or until melted. In shallow pie plate, combine crumb coating ingredients. Dip chicken first in melted margarine and then in crumb mixture, pressing lightly to coat.

In 10-inch skillet, melt remaining 2 tablespoons margarine conventionally over medium heat. Add chicken. Cook for 5 to 7 minutes, or just until brown on both sides. Arrange on serving plate. Sprinkle with shredded cheese. Microwave at High for 45 seconds to 1 minute, or until cheese is melted.

In small bowl, microwave pizza sauce at High for 1½ to 2 minutes, or until hot, stirring once. Serve sauce as dip with chicken strips.

Per Serving: Calories: 148 • Protein: 13 g. • Carbohydrate: 7 g. • Fat: 7 g.
• Cholesterol: 31 mg. • Sodium: 407 mg.
Exchanges: ⅓ starch, 1½ lean meat, ½ vegetable, ½ fat

Idea: **Oriental Chicken Strips with Plum Sauce:** Prepare as directed above, except substitute ½ cup cornflake crumbs, ¼ cup grated Parmesan cheese, ½ teaspoon five-spice powder and ¼ teaspoon garlic powder for crumb coating ingredients. Substitute 1 cup plum preserves, 2 teaspoons grated fresh gingerroot and 1 teaspoon lemon juice for dipping sauce ingredient.

Mustard-Dill Chicken Strips

¼ cup sugar
2 tablespoons dry mustard
1 tablespoon plus 1 teaspoon all-purpose flour
½ teaspoon dried dill weed
¼ teaspoon salt
1 cup milk
¼ cup white vinegar
1 egg yolk
2 boneless whole chicken breasts (8 to 10 oz. each), split in half, skin removed, cut into ¾-inch strips
Fresh dill weed sprigs

8 to 10 servings

In medium mixing bowl, combine sugar, mustard, flour, dill weed and salt. Blend in milk, vinegar and egg yolk. Microwave at High for 3 to 4 minutes, or until sauce thickens and bubbles, stirring after every minute. Cool slightly.

Arrange chicken in even layer in 9-inch cake dish. Pour ¾ cup sauce over chicken. Cover remaining sauce with plastic wrap. Chill. Stir chicken to coat with sauce. Cover with plastic wrap. Chill at least 1 hour.

Drain and discard sauce from chicken. Arrange chicken on rack in broiler pan. Place under conventional broiler with surface of meat 7 inches from heat. Broil for 10 to 15 minutes, or until meat is no longer pink, turning and brushing frequently with ¼ cup reserved sauce.

Place chicken on serving plate. Top each strip with some of remaining sauce and a dill sprig. Serve with remaining sauce.

Per Serving: Calories: 74 • Protein: 11 g. • Carbohydrate: 3 g. • Fat: 2 g.
• Cholesterol: 38 mg. • Sodium: 51 mg.
Exchanges: 1½ lean meat

41

Chicken Caesar Salad

Chicken Almond Salad

Easy Chicken Rotini Salad

Chicken Almond Salad

- 2 boneless whole chicken breasts (8 to 10 oz. each), split in half, skin removed
- ¼ teaspoon seasoned salt or celery salt
- ⅛ to ¼ teaspoon pepper
- ⅛ teaspoon garlic powder
- ½ cup finely chopped celery
- ¼ to ⅓ cup chopped onion

- 2 tablespoons slivered almonds, toasted

Dressing:
- ½ cup mayonnaise or salad dressing mixed with 1 teaspoon prepared or Dijon mustard

4 servings

Place chicken in 8-inch square baking dish. Sprinkle evenly with seasoned salt, pepper and garlic powder. Cover with wax paper or microwave cooking paper. Microwave at High for 4 to 9 minutes, or until meat is no longer pink and juices run clear, rearranging once. Drain. Cool slightly. Cut into ¾-inch pieces. In medium mixing bowl, combine chicken, celery, onion and almonds. Add dressing. Toss to coat. Serve immediately or cover and chill 1 hour.

Per Serving: Calories: 321 • Protein: 21 g. • Carbohydrate: 3 g. • Fat: 25 g.
• Cholesterol: 64 mg. • Sodium: 315 mg.
Exchanges: 2 medium-fat meat, 1 vegetable, 4 fat

Idea: **Creamy Chicken, Corn & Cumin Salad:**
Prepare as directed, except add 1 cup cooked corn and ½ cup chopped red pepper. Substitute ⅓ cup sliced green onions for chopped onion. Omit almonds. Omit mustard from dressing and add 2 tablespoons sour cream, ¼ teaspoon ground cumin and ⅛ teaspoon cayenne.

Creamy Chicken, Corn & Cumin Salad

Southern-style
Chicken Salad

Idea: **Easy Chicken Rotini Salad:** Prepare as directed, except add 2 cups cooked rotini pasta, 1 cup chopped seeded tomato and 1 cup sliced zucchini. Substitute ½ cup sliced green onions for onion. Omit almonds. To dressing, add ¼ cup snipped fresh basil leaves and 1 tablespoon Italian dressing.

Idea: **Southern-style Chicken Salad:** Prepare as directed, except add 1 cup chopped red apple, ⅓ cup chopped dill pickle and 1 or 2 chopped hard-cooked eggs. Omit almonds.

Idea: **A B C Chicken Salad:** Prepare as directed, except omit dressing and add 1 cup cooked mixed vegetables and one 8-oz. pkg. alphabet pasta, cooked. Omit almonds. Substitute ⅔ cup French dressing for dressing ingredients.

Idea: **Waldorf Chicken Salad:** Prepare as directed, except add 1 cup each chopped red and green apple and ½ cup golden raisins. Substitute ½ cup chopped pecans for almonds. Omit mustard from dressing and add ¼ cup defrosted frozen apple juice concentrate and 2 tablespoons sour cream.

A B C Chicken Salad

Waldorf Chicken Salad

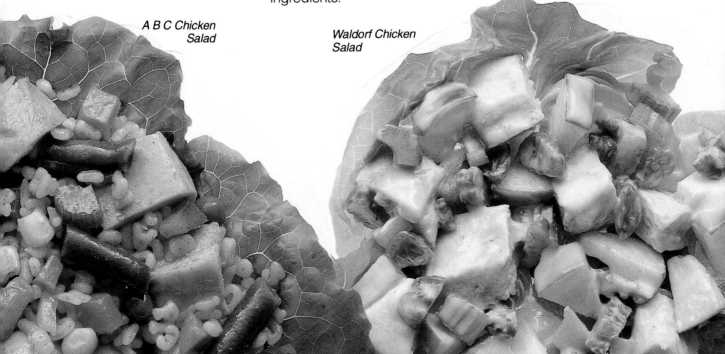

◄ Crunchy Chicken Salad

2 boneless whole chicken breasts (8 to 10 oz.
    each), split in half, skin removed
¼ cup creamy peanut butter
¼ cup mayonnaise
¼ cup honey
1 medium red apple, cored and cut into
    ½-inch chunks
½ cup sliced celery
½ cup raisins
⅓ cup dry-roasted peanuts

4 servings

Place chicken in 8-inch square baking dish. Cover with wax paper or microwave cooking paper. Microwave at High for 4 to 9 minutes, or until meat is no longer pink and juices run clear, rearranging once. Drain. Cool slightly. Cut into ¾-inch pieces. Set aside.

In small mixing bowl, combine peanut butter, mayonnaise and honey. Set aside. In medium mixing bowl, combine chicken, apple, celery, raisins and peanuts. Toss to combine. Add peanut butter mixture. Toss to coat. Serve salad on lettuce-lined serving plates. Garnish with additional chopped dry-roasted peanuts, if desired. Serve immediately.

Per Serving: Calories: 539 • Protein: 34 g. • Carbohydrate: 43 g.
• Fat: 28 g. • Cholesterol: 78 mg. • Sodium: 336 mg.
Exchanges: 1½ high-fat meat, 3 lean meat, 3 fruit, 1½ fat

◄ Fruited Chicken Salad

2 boneless whole chicken breasts (8 to 10 oz.
    each), split in half, skin removed
2 cups halved seedless red and green grapes
1 can (15 oz.) pineapple chunks, drained
½ cup chopped pecans
¼ cup mayonnaise
¼ cup sour cream
1 tablespoon sugar

4 to 6 servings

Place chicken in 8-inch square baking dish. Cover with wax paper or microwave cooking paper. Microwave at High for 4 to 9 minutes, or until meat is no longer pink and juices run clear, rearranging once. Drain. Cool slightly. Cut into ¾-inch pieces.

In large mixing bowl or salad bowl, combine chicken, grapes, pineapple and pecans. In small mixing bowl, combine mayonnaise, sour cream and sugar. Add to chicken mixture. Toss to coat. Serve immediately.

Per Serving: Calories: 316 • Protein: 19 g. • Carbohydrate: 23 g.
• Fat: 18 g. • Cholesterol: 56 mg. • Sodium: 100 mg.
Exchanges: 2½ lean meat, 1½ fruit, 2 fat

Cranberry Chicken & Wild Rice Salad

5 cups water
1½ cups uncooked wild rice
1 teaspoon salt
2 boneless whole chicken
    breasts (8 to 10 oz. each),
    split in half, skin removed

Dressing:

¼ cup vegetable oil
2 tablespoons frozen orange
    juice concentrate,
    defrosted
2 tablespoons red wine
    vinegar
1 tablespoon sugar
1 teaspoon grated orange
    peel
¼ teaspoon salt

1 cup sliced almonds
1 pkg. (12 oz.) fresh or
    frozen cranberries
⅔ cup sugar
1 cup sliced celery

6 to 8 servings

Heat conventional oven to 350°F. In 2-quart saucepan, combine water, rice and salt. Cook conventionally over medium-high heat until boiling. Cover. Reduce heat to low. Cook for 45 to 50 minutes longer, or until rice kernels are open. Drain. Place rice in large mixing bowl or salad bowl. Set aside.

Place chicken in 8-inch square baking dish. Cover with wax paper or microwave cooking paper. Microwave at High for 4 to 9 minutes, or until meat is no longer pink and juices run clear, rearranging once. Drain. Cool slightly. Cut into ¾-inch pieces. Set aside.

In 1-cup measure, combine dressing ingredients. Set aside. Sprinkle almonds in 15½ x 10½ x 1-inch jelly roll pan. Bake conventionally for 3 to 4 minutes, or until lightly browned. Add cranberries. Sprinkle with sugar. Stir to coat cranberries and almonds with sugar. Spread mixture in even layer. Bake for 10 to 12 minutes, or until sugar is melted and cranberries are glazed. Cool slightly. Add chicken, dressing, cranberry mixture and celery to wild rice. Toss to combine. Chill 2 hours, or until cold.

Per Serving: Calories: 406 • Protein: 20 g. • Carbohydrate: 51 g. • Fat: 15 g.
• Cholesterol: 35 mg. • Sodium: 390 mg.
Exchanges: 1½ starch, 2 lean meat, 1½ fruit, 2 fat

Chinese Cabbage & Snow Pea Salad

Dressing:

¼ cup creamy peanut butter
¼ cup water
2 tablespoons peanut oil
2 tablespoons red wine vinegar
1 tablespoon soy sauce
1 teaspoon grated fresh gingerroot

1 tablespoon vegetable oil
1 tablespoon dry sherry
2 teaspoons soy sauce
1 clove garlic, minced
1 teaspoon grated fresh gingerroot
1 teaspoon sugar
⅛ teaspoon pepper
¾ lb. boneless skinless chicken breast tenders
1 cup carrot strips (2 x ¼-inch strips)
½ cup fresh snow pea pods
⅓ cup red pepper chunks (1-inch chunks)
¼ cup sliced green onions
2 tablespoons water
5 cups shredded Chinese cabbage
2 tablespoons chopped dry-roasted peanuts

4 to 6 servings

In 2-cup measure, combine dressing ingredients. Set aside. In 8-inch square baking dish, combine vegetable oil, sherry, soy sauce, garlic, gingerroot, sugar and pepper. Add chicken. Toss to coat. Cover with plastic wrap. Chill 1 hour.

Heat 12-inch nonstick skillet conventionally over medium-high heat. Add chicken. Cook for 5 to 7 minutes, or just until brown on both sides. Cut each piece in half diagonally. Set aside.

In 2-quart casserole, combine carrots, pea pods, red pepper, onions and water. Cover. Microwave at High for 2½ to 3½ minutes, or until vegetables are tender-crisp, stirring once. Drain.

In large mixing bowl or salad bowl, combine chicken, vegetables, cabbage and peanuts. Microwave dressing at High for 1½ to 2½ minutes, or until hot, stirring once. Pour dressing over salad. Toss to coat. Serve immediately.

Per Serving: Calories: 229 • Protein: 18 g. • Carbohydrate: 9 g. • Fat: 14 g. • Cholesterol: 35 mg. • Sodium: 349 mg. Exchanges: 2¼ lean meat, 1½ fat

Stir-fry Chicken & Green Bean Salad

- 2 boneless whole chicken breasts (8 to 10 oz. each), split in half, skin removed
- 2 cloves garlic, minced, divided
- 2 tablespoons soy sauce, divided
- 2 tablespoons vegetable oil, divided
- 1 tablespoon dry sherry
- 1 teaspoon sugar
- ¼ teaspoon pepper, divided
- 4 oz. uncooked capellini (angel hair spaghetti)
- 1 pkg. (9 oz.) frozen French-style green beans
- 1 medium onion, cut into 8 wedges
- 1 cup diagonally sliced carrots
- 1 tablespoon oyster sauce
- 2 tablespoons water
- ⅛ teaspoon crushed red pepper flakes
- ⅛ teaspoon salt

4 servings

Place chicken in 8-inch square baking dish. In small bowl, combine 1 clove garlic, 1 tablespoon soy sauce, 1 tablespoon oil, the sherry, sugar and ⅛ teaspoon pepper. Spoon mixture over chicken. Turn to coat. Cover with plastic wrap. Chill 1 hour. Prepare capellini as directed on package. Rinse and drain. Set aside.

Remove plastic wrap from chicken. Re-cover with wax paper or microwave cooking paper. Microwave at High for 4 to 9 minutes, or until meat is no longer pink and juices run clear, re-arranging once. Drain. Cool slightly. Cut each breast half into thin strips. Set aside.

In 2-quart casserole, combine green beans, onion, carrots, oyster sauce, water, red pepper flakes, salt and remaining clove garlic, 1 tablespoon soy sauce, 1 tablespoon vegetable oil and ⅛ teaspoon pepper. Cover. Microwave at High for 9 to 11 minutes, or until vegetables are tender-crisp, stirring once or twice. In large mixing bowl or salad bowl, combine capellini, chicken and the vegetable mixture. Toss to coat. Serve immediately.

Per Serving: Calories: 360 • Protein: 32 g. • Carbohydrate: 34 g. • Fat: 10 g. • Cholesterol: 70 mg. • Sodium: 838 mg.
Exchanges: 1½ starch, 3 lean meat, 2 vegetable, ¼ fat

Zesty Spaghetti Squash Salad

3½ to 4-lb. whole spaghetti
    squash
  1 cup fresh broccoli
    flowerets
  2 tablespoons water
  2 boneless whole chicken
    breasts (8 to 10 oz. each),
    split in half, skin removed
  2 teaspoons margarine or
    butter
  1 teaspoon Italian seasoning
  ¼ teaspoon salt
  ¼ teaspoon pepper
  5 oz. fresh mushrooms, sliced
    (1¼ cups)
  1 cup halved cherry
    tomatoes
  ½ cup sliced black olives
  ¾ cup Italian dressing

4 servings

Pierce squash rind deeply with sharp knife in several places. Place squash on paper towel in microwave oven. Microwave at High for 12 to 19 minutes, or until squash yields to pressure and feels soft. Let stand for 5 minutes. Cut in half crosswise. Scoop out and discard seeds. Twist out long strands of flesh with fork. Place in large mixing bowl or salad bowl. Set aside. In 1-quart casserole, combine broccoli and water. Cover. Microwave at High for 2 to 4 minutes, or until broccoli is very hot and color brightens. Rinse with cold water. Drain. Set aside.

Place chicken in 8-inch square baking dish. Dot with margarine. Sprinkle evenly with Italian seasoning, salt and pepper. Cover with wax paper or microwave cooking paper. Microwave at High for 4 to 9 minutes, or until meat is no longer pink and juices run clear, re-arranging once. Drain. Cool slightly. Cut into ¾-inch pieces. Add chicken, broccoli and remaining ingredients, except dressing, to squash. Mix well. Add dressing. Toss to coat. Cover with plastic wrap. Chill 2 hours, or until cold.

Per Serving: Calories: 471 • Protein: 29 g. • Carbohydrate: 22 g. • Fat: 32 g.
• Cholesterol: 70 mg. • Sodium: 1225 mg.
Exchanges: 3 lean meat, 4½ vegetable, 4½ fat

   Idea: Reserve hollowed-out squash halves to use as serving bowls for salad. Arrange filled halves on lettuce-lined woven serving tray. Garnish with small whole summer squashes and other fresh vegetables.

   Idea: Spoon salad mixture into hollowed-out tomatoes.

Country Greek Salad

2 boneless whole chicken breasts (8 to 10 oz. each), split in half, skin removed
⅓ cup plus 2 tablespoons Italian dressing, divided
2 cups shredded romaine lettuce
1 can (15 oz.) garbanzo beans, rinsed and drained
1 cup chopped seeded tomato
1 cup crumbled feta cheese
½ cup thinly sliced green pepper
½ cup sliced black olives
½ cup sliced celery
⅓ cup sliced green onions
2 tablespoons snipped fresh oregano leaves

4 to 6 servings

Place chicken in 8-inch square baking dish. Spoon 2 tablespoons Italian dressing over chicken. Turn to coat. Cover with wax paper or microwave cooking paper. Microwave at High for 4 to 9 minutes, or until meat is no longer pink and juices run clear, rearranging once. Drain. Cool slightly. Cut into ¾-inch pieces.

In large mixing bowl or salad bowl, combine chicken, remaining ⅓ cup Italian dressing and remaining ingredients. Toss to coat. Serve immediately.

Per Serving: Calories: 291 • Protein: 24 g. • Carbohydrate: 13 g. • Fat: 16 g. • Cholesterol: 64 mg. • Sodium: 612 mg.
Exchanges: ¾ starch, 3 lean meat, ½ vegetable, 1½ fat

Idea: Salad-stuffed Sourdough: Cut 1½ to 2-inch slice from top of 2-lb. round sourdough bread loaf. Cut circle 1½ inches from outer edge of crust. Remove center, leaving at least 2 inches of bread on bottom. Cut center and top into 1-inch cubes to yield 3 cups. In 10-inch square casserole, microwave 3 tablespoons margarine or butter at High for 1 to 1¼ minutes, or until melted. Add ¼ teaspoon garlic powder. Add bread cubes. Toss to coat. Microwave at High for 6 to 8 minutes, or until bread cubes are crisp, stirring twice. Add to salad. Spoon salad mixture into hollowed-out loaf.

Spicy-Sweet Chicken Salad

Marinade:
- 1 tablespoon vegetable oil
- 1 tablespoon dry sherry
- 1 teaspoon hoisin sauce
- 1 clove garlic, minced
- ½ teaspoon Chinese hot oil
- ½ teaspoon sugar

- 2 boneless whole chicken breasts (8 to 10 oz. each), split in half, skin removed

Dressing:
- 2 tablespoons vegetable oil
- 1 tablespoon hoisin sauce
- 1½ to 2 teaspoons Chinese hot oil
- ½ teaspoon oyster sauce
- ¼ teaspoon five-spice powder

- 2 cups frozen unsweetened sliced peaches
- 8 oz. fresh asparagus spears, diagonally sliced into 2-inch lengths (2 cups)
- 2 tablespoons water
- Cashews (optional)

4 servings

In 8-inch square baking dish, combine marinade ingredients. Add chicken. Turn to coat. Cover with plastic wrap. Chill 2 hours, turning once.

In small mixing bowl, combine dressing ingredients. Set aside. Remove plastic wrap from chicken. Re-cover with wax paper or microwave cooking paper. Microwave at High for 4 to 9 minutes, or until meat is no longer pink and juices run clear, rearranging once. Drain. Cool slightly. Cut into ¾-inch pieces. Set aside.

Place peaches in 1-quart casserole. Cover. Microwave at High for 3 to 4 minutes, or until defrosted, stirring once. Drain. Cut peach slices into thirds. Set aside. In same 1-quart casserole, place asparagus. Add water. Cover. Microwave at High for 5 to 7 minutes, or until tender-crisp, stirring once. Drain.

In large mixing bowl or salad bowl, combine chicken, peaches and asparagus. Add dressing. Toss to coat. Serve on shredded cabbage, if desired. Garnish with cashews.

Per Serving: Calories: 293 • Protein: 29 g. • Carbohydrate: 14 g. • Fat: 14 g. • Cholesterol: 70 mg. • Sodium: 241 mg.
Exchanges: 3 lean meat, 1 vegetable, 1 fruit, 1 fat

Indian Melon & Kiwi Salad

2 boneless whole chicken
   breasts (8 to 10 oz. each),
   split in half, skin removed
½ teaspoon curry powder
1 carton (8 oz.) lemon-flavored
   low-fat yogurt
¼ teaspoon dry mustard
¼ teaspoon salt

3 cups honeydew and
   cantaloupe melon balls
2 kiwifruit, peeled, cut in half
   lengthwise, then crosswise
   into slices
¾ cup golden raisins
½ cup sliced almonds, toasted

4 to 6 servings

Idea: Reserve hollowed-out melon halves to use as serving bowls for salad. Using thin-bladed knife, cut decorative edge (above) on each melon half, or etch decorative design (below), using grooved citrus cutter. Arrange filled melon halves on lettuce-lined serving plates.

Place chicken in 8-inch square baking dish. Sprinkle evenly with curry powder. Cover with wax paper or microwave cooking paper. Microwave at High for 4 to 9 minutes, or until meat is no longer pink and juices run clear, rearranging once. Drain. Cool slightly. Cut into ¾-inch pieces. Set aside.

In large mixing bowl or salad bowl, combine yogurt, mustard and salt. Add chicken and remaining ingredients. Toss to coat.

Per Serving: Calories: 276 • Protein: 22 g. • Carbohydrate: 34 g. • Fat: 7 g.
• Cholesterol: 48 mg. • Sodium: 165 mg.
Exchanges: 2¼ starch, 2 fruit

Tropical Fruit Salad

⅓ cup flaked coconut
¼ cup soy sauce
2 tablespoons dry sherry
2 teaspoons sugar
1 clove garlic, minced
¼ teaspoon ground ginger
¾ lb. boneless skinless
   chicken breast tenders

Dressing:
¼ cup vegetable oil
2 tablespoons frozen orange
   juice concentrate, defrosted
2 tablespoons white wine
   vinegar
2 tablespoons sugar
¼ teaspoon salt

1 fresh mango, cut into
   12 wedges
2 medium bananas, cut
   diagonally into ½-inch slices
2 tablespoons orange or
   lemon juice
2 cups Bibb lettuce, torn into
   bite-size pieces
2 kiwifruit, peeled and cut
   into ½-inch slices

4 to 6 servings

Sprinkle coconut in 9-inch pie plate. Microwave at HIgh for 3 to 4½ minutes, or until lightly browned, tossing with fork after first minute and then every 30 seconds. Set aside. In 8-inch square baking dish, combine soy sauce, sherry, sugar, garlic and ginger. Add chicken. Toss to coat. Cover with plastic wrap. Chill 1 hour.

Remove plastic wrap from chicken. Re-cover with wax paper or microwave cooking paper. Microwave at High for 5 to 6 minutes, or until meat is no longer pink, stirring once. Drain. Set aside.

In 1-cup measure, combine dressing ingredients. Set aside. In medium mixing bowl, combine mango wedges, banana slices and orange juice. Toss to coat. On 12-inch serving plate, arrange lettuce, chicken, mango mixture and kiwi slices. Sprinkle with toasted coconut. Serve with dressing.

Per Serving: Calories: 280 • Protein: 14 g. • Carbohydrate: 30 g. • Fat: 12 g.
• Cholesterol: 35 mg. • Sodium: 492 mg.
Exchanges: 1½ lean meat, 2 fruit, 1½ fat

Idea: Substitute toasted fresh coconut curls (below) for flaked coconut.

Toasted Fresh Coconut Curls: Heat conventional oven to 375°F. Pierce the three shiny black "eyes" at top of coconut with ice pick or screwdriver; drain liquid. Split coconut open by hitting it several times with a hammer. Pull husk away from meat. Using vegetable peeler, remove thin strips of coconut meat. Spread strips evenly on large baking sheet. Bake for 5 to 7 minutes, or until light golden brown, stirring once or twice.

Toasted Coconut Chicken Salad

½ cup flaked coconut
4½ cups water
¾ cup uncooked wild rice
¾ teaspoon salt, divided
2 boneless whole chicken breasts (8 to 10 oz. each), split in half, skin removed
¼ teaspoon white pepper
1 can (11 oz.) pineapple tidbits and mandarin orange segments, drained (reserve 2 tablespoons juice for dressing)
⅓ cup coarsely chopped macadamia nuts (optional)
¼ cup sliced green onions

Dressing:

½ cup mayonnaise
3 tablespoons sugar
2 tablespoons half-and-half
¼ teaspoon white pepper

4 servings

Sprinkle coconut in 9-inch pie plate. Microwave at High for 3 to 4½ minutes, or until lightly browned, tossing with fork after first minute and then every 30 seconds. Set aside.

In 2-quart saucepan, combine water, rice and ½ teaspoon salt. Cook conventionally over medium-high heat until boiling. Cover. Reduce heat to low. Cook for 40 to 45 minutes longer, or until rice kernels are open. Drain. Set aside.

Place chicken in 8-inch square baking dish. Sprinkle evenly with remaining ¼ teaspoon salt and the pepper. Cover with wax paper or microwave cooking paper. Microwave at High for 4 to 9 minutes, or until meat is no longer pink and juices run clear, rearranging once. Drain. Cool slightly. Cut into ¾-inch pieces.

In large mixing bowl or salad bowl, combine rice, chicken, pineapple and orange segments, nuts and onions. Set aside. In small mixing bowl, combine reserved juice, dressing ingredients and 6 tablespoons coconut. Add dressing to chicken mixture. Toss to coat. Cover with plastic wrap. Chill 2 hours, or until cold. Before serving, sprinkle with remaining 2 tablespoons coconut.

Per Serving: Calories: 571 • Protein: 32 g. • Carbohydrate: 50 g. • Fat: 27 g.
• Cholesterol: 85 mg. • Sodium: 675 mg.
Exchanges: 1½ starch, 4 lean meat, 1¾ fruit, 3 fat

Chicken Succotash Salad

6 slices bacon

2 boneless whole chicken breasts (8 to 10 oz. each), split in half, skin removed

2 teaspoons margarine or butter

1/4 teaspoon salt

1/8 teaspoon freshly ground pepper

1/8 teaspoon onion powder

1 pkg. (9 oz.) frozen lima beans

1 cup frozen corn

3/4 cup red pepper strips (2 x 1/4-inch strips)

1/2 cup sliced green onions

Dressing:

2 tablespoons sliced green onion

2 tablespoons all-purpose flour

1/2 cup ready-to-serve chicken broth

1/2 cup half-and-half

1/4 teaspoon salt

1/8 teaspoon freshly ground pepper

1/8 teaspoon onion powder

1 can (15 oz.) black beans, rinsed and drained

4 servings

Arrange bacon on roasting rack. Cover with paper towel. Microwave at High for 5 1/2 to 6 minutes, or until bacon is brown and crisp. Reserve 1 tablespoon drippings. Cool bacon slightly. Cut into 1-inch pieces. Set aside.

Place chicken in 8-inch square baking dish. Dot with margarine. Sprinkle evenly with salt, pepper and onion powder. Cover with wax paper or microwave cooking paper. Microwave at High for 4 to 9 minutes, or until meat is no longer pink and juices run clear, rearranging once. Drain. Cool slightly. Cut into 3/4-inch pieces. Set aside.

In 2-quart casserole, combine lima beans, corn, red pepper strips and onions. Cover. Microwave at High for 6 to 7 minutes, or until vegetables are tender-crisp, stirring once. Set aside. In 2-cup measure, combine reserved bacon drippings and 2 tablespoons onion. Microwave at High for 1 1/2 minutes. Stir in flour. Blend in remaining dressing ingredients. Microwave at High for 6 to 7 minutes, or until dressing thickens and bubbles, stirring 2 or 3 times. In large mixing bowl or salad bowl, combine bacon, chicken, vegetable mixture and beans. Add dressing. Toss to coat. Serve immediately.

Per Serving: Calories: 460 • Protein: 40 g. • Carbohydrate: 37 g. • Fat: 17 g. • Cholesterol: 92 mg. • Sodium: 868 mg.
Exchanges: 2 1/4 starch, 4 lean meat, 1 vegetable, 3/4 fat

Idea: Spoon mixture into center of Golden Corn Bread Ring ▲ (below).

Golden Corn Bread Ring: Heat conventional oven to 400°F. Grease 9-inch (6 1/2-cup) ring pan. Set aside. In medium mixing bowl, combine 1 cup all-purpose flour, 2/3 cup yellow cornmeal, 3 tablespoons sugar and 1 1/2 teaspoons baking powder. Stir in 3/4 cup milk, 3 tablespoons vegetable oil and 1 egg. Pour batter into prepared pan. Bake for 20 to 25 minutes, or until corn bread is light golden brown and wooden pick inserted in center comes out clean. Let stand for 5 minutes. Loosen edges and invert on serving platter.

Smoky Barbecue Chicken Salad

2 boneless whole chicken breasts (8 to 10 oz. each), split in half, skin removed

Marinade:

1 tablespoon vegetable oil
1½ teaspoons liquid smoke
1 tablespoon finely chopped onion
⅛ teaspoon salt
⅛ teaspoon pepper

4 cups torn fresh spinach leaves
½ cup shredded carrot
½ cup thinly sliced red onion rings
1 medium tomato, cut into 8 wedges

Dressing:

¼ cup barbecue sauce
3 tablespoons vegetable oil
2 tablespoons finely chopped onion
1 tablespoon apple cider vinegar
1 tablespoon packed brown sugar
¼ teaspoon liquid smoke

4 servings

Place chicken in 8-inch square baking dish. In small dish, combine marinade ingredients. Spoon mixture over chicken. Turn to coat. Cover with plastic wrap. Chill 1 hour. In large mixing bowl or salad bowl, combine spinach, carrot, red onion rings and tomato wedges. Set aside.

Grill chicken conventionally over medium-high heat for 18 to 20 minutes, or until meat is no longer pink and juices run clear, turning once. Cool slightly. Cut into thin strips. Add to spinach mixture.

In 2-cup measure, combine dressing ingredients. Microwave at High for 1½ to 2 minutes, or until hot, stirring once. Pour dressing over salad. Toss to coat. Serve immediately.

Per Serving: Calories: 301 • Protein: 28 g. • Carbohydrate: 13 g. • Fat: 15 g. • Cholesterol: 70 mg. • Sodium: 276 mg.
Exchanges: 3 lean meat, 2½ vegetable, 1¼ fat

Idea: Spoon mixture into center of Golden Corn Bread Ring (opposite).

Sante Fe Chicken & Potato Salad

1½ lbs. red potatoes, cut into
  ¾-inch cubes
¼ cup plus 2 tablespoons
  water, divided
2 cups frozen corn, red and
  green peppers
2 boneless whole chicken
  breasts (8 to 10 oz. each),
  split in half, skin removed
1 pkg. (1¼ oz.) taco
  seasoning mix, divided
½ cup mayonnaise
½ cup sour cream
½ cup salsa
1 can (15½ oz.) kidney beans,
  rinsed and drained
1 cup shredded Cheddar
  cheese
1 can (4 oz.) sliced black olives,
  rinsed and drained

4 to 6 servings

In 2-quart casserole, combine potatoes and ¼ cup water. Cover. Microwave at High for 8 to 12 minutes, or until potatoes are tender, stirring once or twice. Rinse with cold water. Drain. Set aside.

In same 2-quart casserole, combine corn mixture and remaining 2 tablespoons water. Cover. Microwave at High for 3 to 5 minutes, or until corn is defrosted, stirring once. Rinse with cold water. Drain. Set aside.

Place chicken in 8-inch square baking dish. Sprinkle evenly with 1 tablespoon taco seasoning mix. Cover with wax paper or micro-wave cooking paper. Microwave at High for 4 to 9 minutes, or until meat is no longer pink and juices run clear, rearranging once. Drain. Cool slightly. Cut into ¾-inch pieces. Set aside.

In small mixing bowl, combine mayonnaise, sour cream, salsa and remaining taco seasoning mix. In large mixing bowl or salad bowl, combine potatoes, corn mixture, chicken, beans and cheese. Add mayonnaise mixture. Toss to coat. Garnish with olives.

Per Serving: Calories: 570 • Protein: 31 g. • Carbohydrate: 46 g. • Fat: 30 g.
• Cholesterol: 86 mg. • Sodium: 1019 mg.
Exchanges: 3 starch, 3 lean meat, 4 fat

  Idea: Serve salad in lettuce-lined crisp flour tortilla bowls.

Minted Chicken Salad

6 oz. uncooked fusilli or rotini pasta (2 cups)
2 boneless whole chicken breasts (8 to 10 oz. each), split in half, skin removed
1 tablespoon plus 2 teaspoons margarine or butter, divided
¼ teaspoon plus ⅛ teaspoon seasoned salt, divided
⅛ teaspoon white pepper

Dressing:

¾ cup sour cream
¼ cup mayonnaise
2 tablespoons fresh lemon juice
2 teaspoons sugar
¼ teaspoon salt
⅛ teaspoon white pepper

2 cups frozen whole baby carrots
1 tablespoon water
1 cup frozen peas
½ cup snipped fresh mint leaves
1 tablespoon snipped fresh chives

4 servings

Cook pasta as directed on package. Rinse with cold water. Drain. Set aside. Place chicken in 8-inch square baking dish. Dot with 2 teaspoons margarine. Sprinkle evenly with ¼ teaspoon seasoned salt and the pepper. Cover with wax paper or microwave cooking paper. Microwave at High for 4 to 9 minutes, or until meat is no longer pink and juices run clear, rearranging once. Drain. Cool slightly. Cut into ¾-inch pieces. Set aside.

In small bowl, combine dressing ingredients. Set aside. In 2-quart casserole, combine carrots, water, remaining 1 tablespoon margarine and ⅛ teaspoon seasoned salt. Cover. Microwave at High for 6 to 8 minutes, or until carrots are tender, stirring once. Add peas. Re-cover. Microwave at High for 1 to 2 minutes, or until hot, stirring once. Drain. Cool slightly.

In large mixing bowl or salad bowl, combine pasta, chicken, vegetables, mint and chives. Add dressing. Toss to coat. Cover with plastic wrap. Chill 2 hours, or until cold.

Per Serving: Calories: 607 • Protein: 36 g. • Carbohydrate: 51 g. • Fat: 29 g. • Cholesterol: 97 mg. • Sodium: 560 mg.
Exchanges: 2½ starch, 3 lean meat, 3 vegetable, 4 fat

Cajun Chicken Salad

2 boneless whole chicken breasts (8 to 10 oz. each), split in half, skin removed
1 tablespoon vegetable oil
¾ teaspoon Cajun seasoning, divided
¼ teaspoon salt
¾ teaspoon freshly ground pepper, divided
1 cup uncooked converted white rice
1 tablespoon instant chicken bouillon granules
1 clove garlic, minced
2 teaspoons margarine or butter
¼ teaspoon dried thyme leaves
2 cups hot water
1 cup red pepper chunks (1-inch chunks)
1 medium onion, cut into 8 wedges
¾ cup sliced celery

6 servings

Place chicken in 8-inch square baking dish. In small bowl, combine oil, ½ teaspoon Cajun seasoning, the salt and ¼ teaspoon pepper. Spoon mixture over chicken. Turn to coat. Cover with plastic wrap. Chill 1 hour.

Remove plastic wrap from chicken. Grill chicken conventionally over medium-high heat for 18 to 20 minutes, or until meat is no longer pink and juices run clear, turning once. Cool slightly. Cut into thin strips. Set aside.

In 10-inch square casserole, combine rice, bouillon, garlic, margarine, remaining ¼ teaspoon Cajun seasoning and ½ teaspoon pepper, and the thyme. Stir in hot water. Cover. Microwave at High for 5 minutes. Stir rice mixture. Re-cover. Microwave at 50% (Medium) for 10 minutes longer.

Stir in red pepper chunks, onion and celery. Re-cover. Microwave at High for 5 to 8 minutes, or until rice is tender and liquid is absorbed, stirring once. Let stand, covered, for 2 minutes. Spoon rice mixture over center of large serving platter. Arrange chicken strips on rice, or toss together. Serve warm.

Per Serving: Calories: 254 • Protein: 20 g. • Carbohydrate: 28 g. • Fat: 6 g.
• Cholesterol: 47 mg. • Sodium: 747 mg.
Exchanges: 1½ starch, 2 lean meat, 1 vegetable

◄ Fried Chicken Salad with Citrus Cilantro Dressing

Dressing:
1 teaspoon grated orange peel
¼ cup fresh orange juice
¼ cup lime juice
¼ cup vegetable oil
¼ cup snipped fresh cilantro leaves
¼ teaspoon salt

1 egg, beaten
1½ teaspoons red pepper sauce
¼ cup yellow cornmeal
¼ teaspoon paprika
¼ teaspoon seasoned salt
2 boneless whole chicken breasts (8 to 10 oz. each), split in half, skin removed
2 tablespoons vegetable oil
4 medium seedless oranges
4 cups fresh spinach leaves
1⅓ cups shredded jicama
1 small red onion, thinly sliced and separated into rings

4 servings

In 2-cup measure, combine dressing ingredients. Set aside. In 1-quart casserole, beat together egg and red pepper sauce. In 9-inch pie plate, combine cornmeal, paprika and seasoned salt. Dip both sides of chicken first in egg mixture and then in cornmeal mixture, pressing lightly to coat.

In 10-inch nonstick skillet, heat oil conventionally over medium-high heat. Add coated chicken. Cook for 7 to 9 minutes, or until brown on both sides, meat is no longer pink and juices run clear, turning twice. Cover to keep warm. Set aside.

Using sharp knife, cut peel and white membrane from oranges. Slice oranges crosswise into ¼-inch slices. Arrange orange slices, spinach, jicama and red onion slices evenly on 4 individual serving plates. Slice each breast half into 6 pieces. Arrange 1 sliced breast half on each serving plate. Microwave dressing mixture at High for 1 to 2 minutes, or until hot, stirring once. Serve with salad.

Per Serving: Calories: 409 • Protein: 32 g. • Carbohydrate: 34 g. • Fat: 17 g.
• Cholesterol: 119 mg. • Sodium: 400 mg.
Exchanges: ½ starch, 3¼ lean meat, 1½ vegetable, 1¼ fruit, 1½ fat

Spinach & Garlic Pesto Pasta

⅓ cup olive oil
1 teaspoon grated lemon peel
3 tablespoons fresh lemon juice, divided
1 to 2 cloves garlic, minced
⅓ cup pine nuts
8 oz. uncooked medium shell pasta (3 cups)
2 cups frozen cut-leaf spinach
2 tablespoons water
2 boneless whole chicken breasts (8 to 10 oz. each), split in half, skin removed
¼ teaspoon garlic powder
½ cup unseasoned dry bread crumbs
⅓ cup grated Parmesan cheese

4 to 6 servings

In 1-cup measure, combine oil, peel, 2 tablespoons juice and the garlic. Set dressing aside. Place pine nuts in 8-inch nonstick skillet. Cook conventionally over medium-high heat for 2 to 4 minutes, or until golden brown, stirring constantly. Set aside. Prepare pasta as directed on package. Rinse and drain. Set aside.

In 1½-quart casserole, combine spinach and water. Cover. Microwave at High for 3 to 4 minutes, or until mixture is hot. Drain, pressing to remove excess moisture. Set aside.

Place chicken in 8-inch square baking dish. Sprinkle with remaining 1 tablespoon juice and the garlic powder. Cover with wax paper or microwave cooking paper. Microwave at High for 4 to 9 minutes, or until meat is no longer pink and juices run clear, rearranging once. Drain. Cool slightly. Cut into ¾-inch pieces.

In large mixing bowl or salad bowl, combine pasta, spinach, chicken, bread crumbs and Parmesan cheese. Add dressing and pine nuts. Toss to coat.

Per Serving: Calories: 450 • Protein: 29 g. • Carbohydrate: 39 g. • Fat: 20 g.
• Cholesterol: 51 mg. • Sodium: 240 mg.
Exchanges: 2¼ starch, 2½ lean meat, ½ vegetable, 2½ fat

Roasted Red Pepper & Pesto Salad

2 boneless whole chicken breasts (8 to 10 oz. each), split in half, skin removed
1¼ cups fresh basil leaves, divided
3 tablespoons olive oil, divided
1 tablespoon lemon juice
½ teaspoon salt, divided
¼ teaspoon white pepper, divided
¼ cup pine nuts, divided
5 oz. uncooked linguine, broken into thirds
1 clove garlic, thinly sliced
¼ cup margarine or butter, softened
¼ cup grated Parmesan cheese
¾ cup canned roasted red peppers, drained, cut into strips

4 servings

Place chicken in 8-inch square baking dish. Chop ¼ cup basil leaves. In small bowl, combine chopped basil, 1 tablespoon oil, the juice, ¼ teaspoon salt and ⅛ teaspoon pepper. Spoon mixture over chicken. Turn to coat. Cover with plastic wrap. Chill 30 minutes.

Place 2 tablespoons pine nuts in 8-inch nonstick skillet. Cook conventionally over medium-high heat for 2 to 4 minutes, or until golden brown, stirring constantly. Set aside. Prepare linguine as directed on package. Rinse and drain. Set aside.

Remove plastic wrap from chicken. Grill chicken conventionally over medium-high heat for 18 to 20 minutes, or until meat is no longer pink and juices run clear, turning once. Cool slightly. Cut into bite-size pieces. Set aside.

In food processor or blender, combine remaining 1 cup basil leaves, 2 tablespoons oil and 2 tablespoons pine nuts, the garlic, margarine and Parmesan cheese. Process until smooth. Set pesto aside.

In large mixing bowl or microwave-safe salad bowl, combine chicken, toasted pine nuts, linguine, remaining ¼ teaspoon salt and ⅛ teaspoon pepper and the red pepper strips. Add pesto. Toss to coat. Microwave salad at 70% (Medium High) for 3 to 5 minutes, or until warm, stirring once. Serve immediately.

Per Serving: Calories: 554 • Protein: 36 g. • Carbohydrate: 34 g. • Fat: 31 g.
• Cholesterol: 74 mg. • Sodium: 576 mg.
Exchanges: 1¾ starch, 4 lean meat, 1 vegetable, 3¾ fat

Hot Ratatouille Salad

3 tablespoons olive oil, divided
1 tablespoon plus 1 teaspoon snipped fresh rosemary leaves, divided
2 cloves garlic, minced, divided
¼ plus ⅛ teaspoon salt, divided
¾ lb. boneless skinless chicken breast tenders
2½ cups cubed eggplant (1-inch cubes)
¾ cup sliced zucchini
½ cup green pepper strips (2½ x ¼-inch strips)
⅓ cup water
½ cup thinly sliced green onions
¼ teaspoon freshly ground pepper

3 to 4 servings

In 8-inch square baking dish, combine 2 tablespoons oil, 1 tablespoon rosemary, 1 clove garlic and ¼ teaspoon salt. Add chicken. Toss to coat. Cover with plastic wrap. Chill 1 hour.

Heat 12-inch nonstick skillet conventionally over medium-high heat. Add chicken. Cook for 5 to 7 minutes, or just until brown on both sides. Set aside.

In 2-quart casserole, combine eggplant, zucchini, green pepper, water and remaining 1 teaspoon rosemary. Cover. Microwave at High for 6 to 8 minutes, or until vegetables are tender-crisp, stirring once. Drain. Set aside.

Using slotted spoon, lift chicken tenders from skillet. Set aside. To drippings in skillet, add remaining 1 tablespoon oil. Heat conventionally over medium-high heat. Add remaining 1 clove garlic and the onions. Cook for 1 to 2 minutes, or until onions are tender, stirring constantly. Add eggplant mixture and chicken. Reduce heat to low. Cook for 1 to 2 minutes, or until hot. Sprinkle with remaining ⅛ teaspoon salt and the pepper. Serve immediately.

Per Serving: Calories: 187 • Protein: 20 g. • Carbohydrate: 6 g. • Fat: 9 g.
• Cholesterol: 53 mg. • Sodium: 152 mg.
Exchanges: 2 lean meat, 1 vegetable, 1 fat

Idea: **Ratatouille Pasta Salad:** Toss salad with 8 oz. hot ▼ cooked ziti or mostaccioli pasta. Serve warm.

Idea: **Ratatouille Pizzas:** Spoon salad mixture evenly onto six 6-inch toasted pita bread rounds. Arrange on large baking sheet. Sprinkle each with 2 tablespoons shredded mozzarella cheese. Place under conventional broiler with surface of pitas 5 to 6 inches from heat. Broil for 3 to 3½ minutes, or until cheese is melted. Serve immediately. ▼

Light & Healthy Brown Rice Salad

Dressing:

- ½ cup mayonnaise
- ¼ cup snipped fresh basil leaves
- 2 tablespoons milk
- 2 teaspoons lemon juice
- 1 teaspoon sugar
- ¼ teaspoon salt

- 3¾ cups water, divided
- 1½ cups uncooked brown rice
- ½ teaspoon salt
- 2 boneless whole chicken breasts (8 to 10 oz. each), split in half, skin removed
- ¼ cup snipped fresh basil leaves
- 1 tablespoon lemon juice
- 1½ cups diagonally sliced carrots
- 2 cups alfalfa sprouts
- 1 cup thinly sliced red pepper

4 to 6 servings

Per Serving: Calories: 423 • Protein: 22 g.
• Carbohydrate: 42 g. • Fat: 18 g.
• Cholesterol: 58 mg. • Sodium: 435 mg.
Exchanges: 2¼ starch, 2 lean meat,
1 vegetable, 2½ fat

In small mixing bowl, combine dressing ingredients. Cover with plastic wrap. Chill. In 2-quart saucepan, combine 3½ cups water, the rice and salt. Cook conventionally over medium-high heat until boiling. Cover. Reduce heat to low. Cook for 40 to 50 minutes, or until rice is tender and liquid is absorbed. Rinse with cold water. Drain. Set aside.

Place chicken in 8-inch square baking dish. Sprinkle evenly with basil and juice. Cover with wax paper or microwave cooking paper. Microwave at High for 4 to 9 minutes, or until meat is no longer pink and juices run clear, rearranging once. Drain. Cool slightly. Cut into ¾-inch pieces. Set aside.

In 2-quart casserole, combine carrots and remaining ¼ cup water. Cover. Microwave at High for 2 to 3 minutes, or until tender-crisp, stirring once. Rinse with cold water. Drain. In large mixing bowl or salad bowl, combine rice, chicken, carrots, sprouts and red pepper. Add dressing. Toss to coat. Sprinkle with freshly ground pepper, if desired.

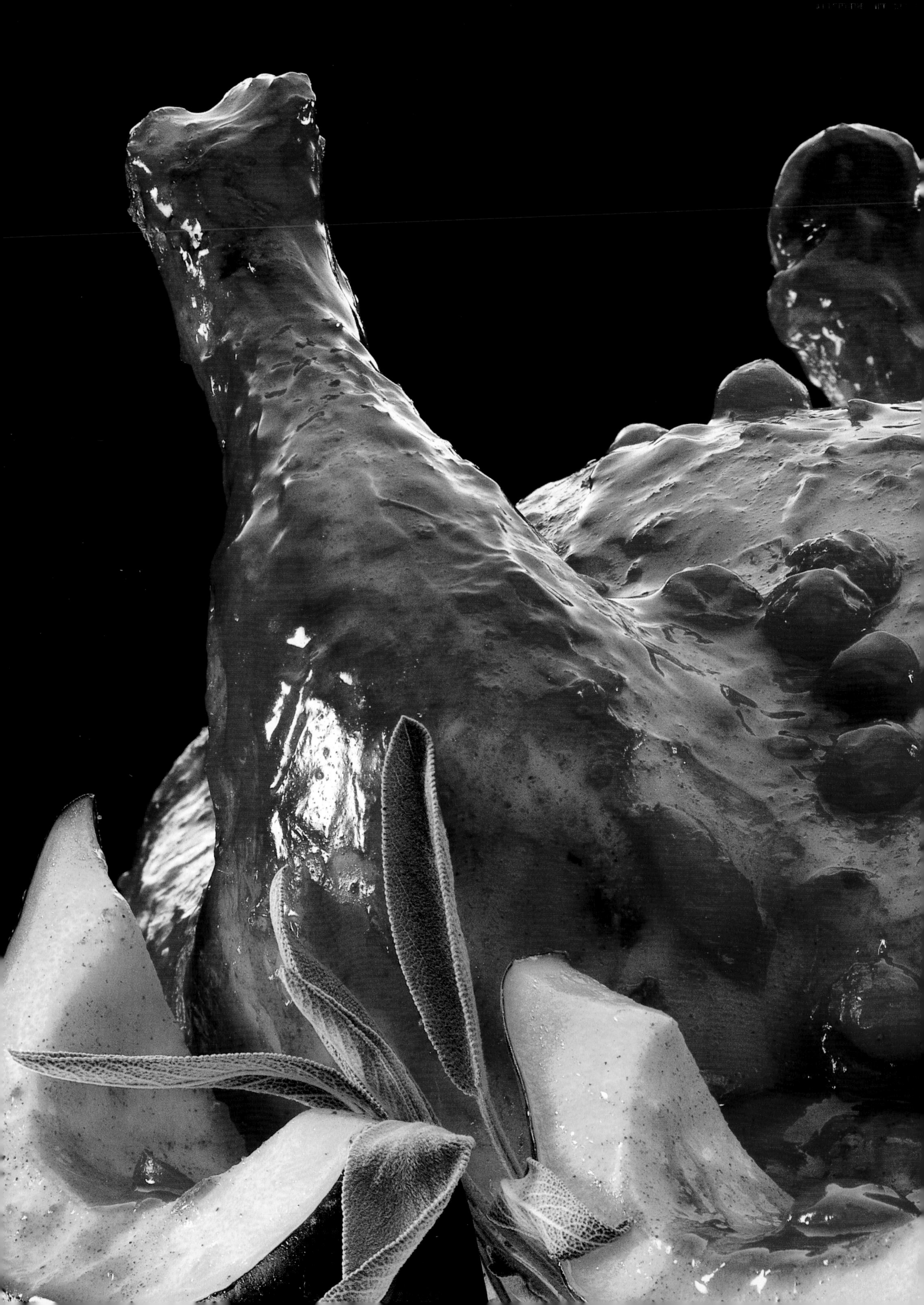

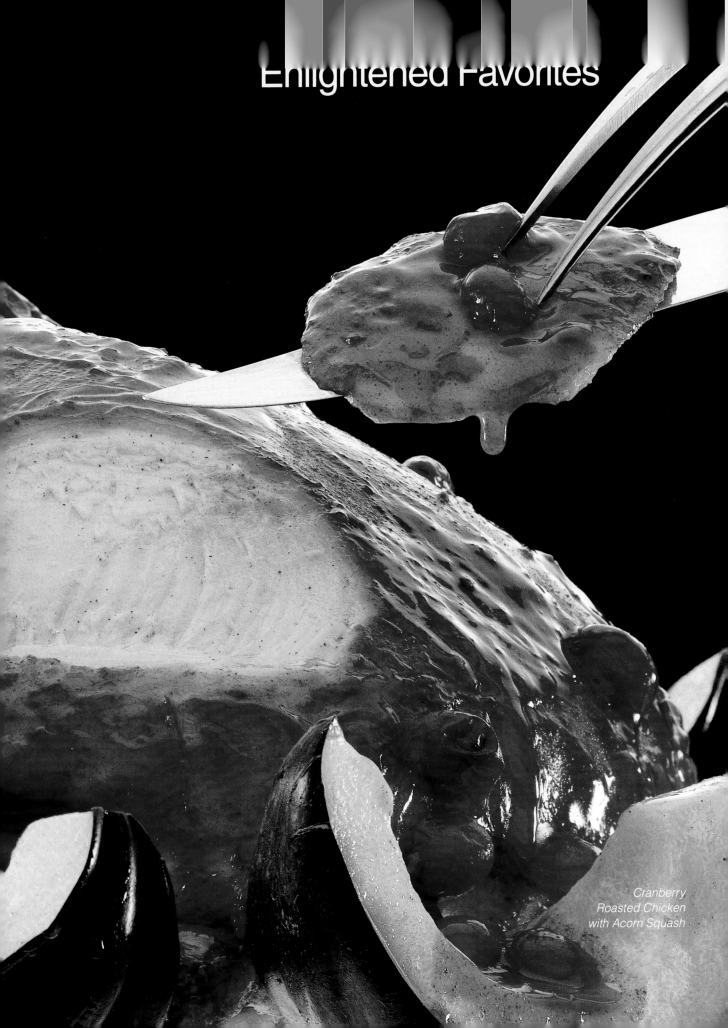

*Cranberry
Roasted Chicken
with Acorn Squash*

Chicken à la King ▶

2 boneless whole chicken breasts (8 to 10 oz. each), split in half, skin removed, cut into ¾-inch pieces
⅓ cup sliced green onions
¼ teaspoon seasoned salt
¼ teaspoon pepper, divided
2 tablespoons cornstarch
¼ teaspoon dried thyme leaves
¼ teaspoon dry mustard
1 cup skim milk
¾ cup low-sodium ready-to-serve chicken broth, defatted*
1½ cups frozen mixed vegetables

6 servings

In 10-inch square casserole, combine chicken, onions, seasoned salt and ⅛ teaspoon pepper. Cover. Microwave at High for 5 to 8 minutes, or until meat is no longer pink, stirring once. Drain. Set aside.

In 4-cup measure, combine cornstarch, thyme, mustard and remaining ⅛ teaspoon pepper. Blend in milk and broth. Microwave at High for 5 to 7 minutes, or until sauce is thickened and translucent, stirring 2 or 3 times.

Add sauce and vegetables to chicken in casserole. Mix well. Cover. Microwave at High for 4 to 6 minutes, or until mixture is hot and vegetables are tender-crisp, stirring once. Serve over split baking powder biscuits or corn muffins, baked potatoes, toast points or hot cooked rice or noodles, if desired.

*Defat broth by chilling 4 hours; skim and discard solidified fat from surface.

Per Serving: Calories: 149 • Protein: 20 g. • Carbohydrate: 11 g. • Fat: 2 g. • Cholesterol: 47 mg. • Sodium: 140 mg.
Exchanges: ½ starch, 2 lean meat, ¼ skim milk

Idea: **Burritos à la King:** Prepare chicken as directed. Prepare sauce as directed, substituting dried oregano leaves for thyme. Omit mixed vegetables. Add 1 can (15 oz.) rinsed and drained pinto beans, 1 can (4 oz.) drained chopped green chilies, ¾ cup frozen corn and the sauce to chicken. Microwave as directed. Serve mixture wrapped in flour tortillas. Garnish with chopped seeded tomato, sliced green onions, shredded lettuce, salsa and shredded reduced-fat Cheddar cheese, if desired.

Idea: **Crepes à la King:** Prepare chicken
▼ as directed. Prepare sauce as directed, substituting ¼ teaspoon dried bouquet garni seasoning and ¼ teaspoon garlic powder for thyme. Microwave as directed. Serve mixture over rolled-up crepes. Sprinkle with finely shredded reduced-fat Cheddar cheese, if desired.

Idea: Mushroom à la King: Prepare chicken as directed. Prepare sauce as directed, substituting 2 teaspoons Worcestershire sauce for thyme. Omit mixed vegetables. Add 1½ cups sliced fresh mushrooms, ¾ cup frozen corn, 2 tablespoons sliced pimiento and the sauce to chicken. Microwave as directed. Serve over hot cooked wild rice.

Idea: Italian à la King Casserole: Prepare chicken as directed. Prepare sauce as directed, substituting Italian seasoning for thyme. Omit mixed vegetables. Add 2 cups frozen broccoli cuts, 1 cup chopped red pepper, 2 cups hot cooked macaroni and the sauce to chicken. Cover. Microwave at High for 6 to 9 minutes, or until mixture is hot and vegetables are tender-crisp, stirring once.

Chow Mein Pizza

½ cup sliced celery
½ cup chopped carrot
1 lb. ground chicken, crumbled
1 cup halved fresh snow pea pods
½ cup chopped red pepper
⅓ cup sliced green onions
1 teaspoon cornstarch
1 teaspoon sugar
¼ teaspoon ground ginger
¼ teaspoon garlic powder
Dash cayenne
2 tablespoons reduced-sodium soy sauce
1 pkg. (10 oz.) refrigerated pizza crust dough
1 cup shredded reduced-fat mozzarella cheese (3 g. fat per oz.)

8 servings

Heat conventional oven to 425°F. In 10-inch square casserole, combine celery and carrot. Cover. Microwave at High for 3 to 4 minutes, or until vegetables are tender-crisp, stirring once. Drain. Remove vegetable mixture from casserole. Set aside.

In same casserole, microwave chicken at High for 4 to 6 minutes, or until meat is no longer pink, stirring once or twice to break apart. Drain. Add vegetable mixture back to casserole. Add pea pods, red pepper and onions. Mix well. Set aside.

In small mixing bowl, combine cornstarch, sugar, ginger, garlic powder and cayenne. Blend in soy sauce. Microwave at High for 30 to 45 seconds, or until mixture is thickened and translucent. Add to chicken mixture. Mix well. Microwave at High for 1 to 3 minutes, or until mixture is hot.

Spray 12-inch pizza pan with nonstick vegetable cooking spray. Press pizza crust over bottom and up sides to form edge. Bake conventionally for 8 to 10 minutes, or until light golden brown. Spoon chicken mixture evenly over crust. Sprinkle with cheese. Bake for 10 to 13 minutes, or until cheese is melted and crust is deep golden brown.

Per Serving: Calories: 228 • Protein: 18 g. • Carbohydrate: 21 g. • Fat: 8 g.
• Cholesterol: 52 mg. • Sodium: 451 mg.
Exchanges: 1 starch, 2 lean meat, 1 vegetable

Chicken Dijon Stroganoff

2 boneless whole chicken breasts (8 to 10 oz. each), split in half, skin removed, cut into 1/2-inch strips

2 cups fresh broccoli flowerets

1 1/2 cups carrot strips (1 1/2 x 1/8-inch strips)

1 medium onion, thinly sliced and separated into rings

1/4 cup all-purpose flour

1/4 teaspoon dried thyme leaves

1/8 teaspoon white pepper

1 1/4 cups low-sodium ready-to-serve chicken broth, defatted*

2 tablespoons Dijon mustard

2 teaspoons honey

1 teaspoon low-sodium Worcestershire sauce

1/3 cup light sour cream

4 to 6 servings

In 10-inch square casserole, combine chicken, broccoli, carrots and onion. Cover. Microwave at High for 8 to 12 minutes, or until meat is no longer pink, stirring twice. Drain. Set aside.

In 4-cup measure, combine flour, thyme and pepper. Blend in broth, mustard, honey and Worcestershire sauce. Microwave at High for 4 to 5 minutes, or until mixture thickens and bubbles, stirring twice.

Pour over chicken mixture. Mix well. Cover. Microwave at High for 3 to 5 minutes, or until hot. Stir in sour cream. Serve over hot cooked rice or noodles, if desired.

*Defat broth by chilling 4 hours; skim and discard solidified fat from surface.

Per Serving: Calories: 183 • Protein: 21 g.
• Carbohydrate: 14 g. • Fat: 5 g.
• Cholesterol: 51 mg. • Sodium: 232 mg.
Exchanges: 1/4 starch, 2 lean meat, 2 vegetable

Chilly Burritos ▲

8 boneless skinless chicken thighs (2 to 3 oz. each), cut into 1/2-inch strips

2 teaspoons vegetable oil

1/2 teaspoon ground cumin, divided

1/4 teaspoon chili powder

1/4 teaspoon salt (optional)

1 can (15 oz.) black beans, rinsed and drained

1 can (8 oz.) tomato sauce

3/4 cup chopped onion, divided

1/2 cup red pepper strips (2 x 1/4-inch strips)

1 can (4 oz.) chopped green chilies

1/2 cup frozen corn

1/4 cup chopped green pepper

1 cup chopped seeded tomato

1 tablespoon fresh lime juice

1/4 teaspoon crushed red pepper flakes

6 flour tortillas (10-inch)

6 servings

In 2-quart casserole, combine chicken, oil, 1/4 teaspoon cumin, the chili powder and salt. Cover with wax paper or microwave cooking paper. Microwave at High for 5 to 7 minutes, or until meat is no longer pink, stirring once. Drain. Shred chicken and return to casserole. Stir in beans, tomato sauce, 1/2 cup onion, the pepper strips and chilies. Re-cover. Microwave at High for 4 to 6 minutes, or until onion and pepper are tender-crisp, stirring once. Chill.

In 1-quart casserole, combine remaining 1/4 teaspoon cumin and 1/4 cup onion, the corn and green pepper. Cover. Microwave at High for 3 to 4 minutes, or until onion and pepper are tender-crisp, stirring once. Stir in tomato, juice and pepper flakes. Chill salsa. Spread heaping 3/4 cup chicken mixture down center of each tortilla. Fold tortilla to completely enclose chicken mixture. Place burritos on plate, seam-side-down. Spoon salsa evenly over each burrito.

Per Serving: Calories: 326 • Protein: 26 g. • Carbohydrate: 41 g. • Fat: 6 g.
• Cholesterol: 78 mg. • Sodium: 754 mg.
Exchanges: 2 starch, 2 1/4 lean meat, 2 vegetable

Greek Phyllo Quiche

1 boneless whole chicken breast (8 to 10 oz.), split in half, skin removed, cut into 1/2-inch pieces
1/2 cup chopped onion
1 tablespoon dried parsley flakes
2 teaspoons olive oil
1 teaspoon dried dill weed
1 clove garlic, minced
1/2 teaspoon grated lemon peel
1/4 teaspoon pepper
1 cup frozen cut-leaf spinach, defrosted
1 carton (8 oz.) frozen cholesterol-free egg product, defrosted
2/3 cup evaporated skim milk
1/3 cup crumbled feta cheese
9 sheets frozen phyllo dough (18 × 14-inch sheets), defrosted and trimmed to 12-inch squares
3 tablespoons margarine or butter, melted

4 to 6 servings

Heat conventional oven to 375°F. In 2-quart casserole, combine chicken, onion, parsley, oil, dill, garlic, peel and pepper. Cover with wax paper or microwave cooking paper. Microwave at High for 4 to 5 minutes, or until meat is no longer pink, stirring once. Drain. Set aside.

Drain spinach, pressing to remove excess moisture. Add spinach, egg product, milk and cheese to chicken mixture. Mix well. Cover. Set aside.

Unroll phyllo sheets. Cover with plastic wrap. Working quickly, brush 1 sheet lightly with margarine and place it in 9-inch pie plate with corners hanging over. Repeat brushing and layering with 4 more sheets. Pour chicken mixture into pie plate. Fold ends of phyllo up and over filling so corners overlap on top.

Brush and layer remaining 4 sheets of phyllo. Place on top of pie to make top crust. Fold edges under, between bottom crust of phyllo and rim of plate, to seal. With sharp knife or scissors, cut top layers of phyllo to make serving-size portions. Bake conventionally for 40 to 45 minutes, or until knife comes out clean when inserted in center and phyllo is golden brown.

Per Serving: Calories: 278 • Protein: 20 g. • Carbohydrate: 27 g. • Fat: 10 g. • Cholesterol: 31 mg. • Sodium: 411 mg.
Exchanges: 1 1/3 starch, 1 1/2 lean meat, 1 vegetable, 1/4 skim milk, 1 fat

Brandied Coq au Vin

1 slice bacon, finely chopped
3 - lb. whole broiler-fryer chicken, cut into 8 pieces, skin removed
1 medium onion, thinly sliced and separated into rings
3 tablespoons all-purpose flour
1/4 teaspoon salt (optional)
1/4 teaspoon dried bouquet garni seasoning
1/4 teaspoon white pepper
1 cup water
1/4 cup dry white wine
1 tablespoon brandy
8 oz. fresh mushrooms, cut into quarters (2 cups)
1/2 cup frozen peas

6 servings

In 12-inch nonstick skillet, cook bacon conventionally over medium-high heat until brown and crisp, stirring constantly. Remove bacon from skillet. Set aside.

Add chicken to skillet. Cook for 4 to 6 minutes, or just until brown on both sides. Remove from heat. Cover to keep warm. Set aside.

Place onion in 8-inch square baking dish. Cover with wax paper or microwave cooking paper. Microwave at High for 3 to 5 minutes, or until tender-crisp, stirring once. Stir in flour, salt, bouquet garni and pepper. Blend in water, wine and brandy. Microwave at High, uncovered, for 3 to 5 minutes, or until sauce thickens and bubbles, stirring once or twice.

Arrange chicken over sauce with thickest portions toward outside. Spoon some of sauce over chicken. Cover with wax paper or microwave cooking paper. Microwave at High for 10 to 15 minutes, or until meat near bone is no longer pink and juices run clear, rearranging and turning chicken over once. Remove chicken from baking dish and place on serving platter. Cover to keep warm. Set aside.

To sauce in baking dish, add mushrooms and peas. Microwave at High, uncovered, for 1 1/2 to 3 minutes, or until mushrooms are tender and sauce is hot, stirring once. Spoon sauce over chicken. Sprinkle with bacon.

Per Serving: Calories: 189 • Protein: 26 g. • Carbohydrate: 8 g. • Fat: 6 g. • Cholesterol: 79 mg. • Sodium: 216 mg.
Exchanges: 1/3 starch, 3 lean meat, 1/2 vegetable

Orange Chicken Véronique

- 1 tablespoon vegetable oil
- 3 - lb. whole broiler-fryer chicken, cut into 8 pieces, skin removed
- 1 tablespoon cornstarch
- 1 teaspoon sugar
- 1/4 teaspoon salt (optional)
- 1/4 teaspoon dried marjoram leaves
- 1/8 teaspoon white pepper
- 1/2 cup orange juice
- 1/4 cup dry white wine
- 1/2 cup halved seedless green grapes
- 1/2 cup halved seedless red grapes
- 1 teaspoon grated orange peel

6 servings

In 12-inch nonstick skillet, heat oil conventionally over medium-high heat. Add chicken. Cook for 4 to 6 minutes, or just until brown on both sides. Remove from heat. Set aside.

In 2-cup measure, combine cornstarch, sugar, salt, marjoram and pepper. Blend in juice and wine. Microwave at High for 4 to 6 minutes, or until sauce is thickened and translucent, stirring twice.

In 10-inch square casserole, arrange chicken with thickest portions toward outside. Pour sauce evenly over chicken. Cover. Microwave at High for 10 to 15 minutes, or until meat near bone is no longer pink and juices run clear, rearranging and turning chicken over once. Remove chicken from casserole and place on serving platter. Cover to keep warm. Set aside.

To sauce in casserole, add grapes and peel. Microwave at High for 1 to 2 minutes, or until sauce is hot. Spoon over chicken.

Per Serving: Calories: 188 • Protein: 24 g. • Carbohydrate: 8 g. • Fat: 6 g. • Cholesterol: 76 mg. • Sodium: 175 mg.
Exchanges: 3 lean meat, 1/2 fruit

Oriental Chicken & Dumplings

½ cup dried shiitake mushrooms
½ cup diagonally sliced green onions (1-inch lengths)
1 tablespoon grated fresh gingerroot
1 clove garlic, minced
3-lb. whole broiler-fryer chicken, cut into 8 pieces, skin removed
1 can (14½ oz.) low-sodium ready-to-serve chicken broth, defatted*
2 tablespoons reduced-sodium soy sauce
¼ teaspoon freshly ground pepper
⅛ teaspoon five-spice powder
3 tablespoons cornstarch mixed with 2 tablespoons water
2 cups frozen broccoli, carrots, water chestnuts and red pepper
1 cup buttermilk baking mix
⅓ cup skim milk
1 tablespoon sesame seed, toasted

4 servings

Rehydrate mushrooms as directed on package. Drain and coarsely chop. Set aside. In 3-quart casserole, combine onions, gingerroot and garlic. Cover. Microwave at High for 2 to 3 minutes, or until onions are tender, stirring once. Add chicken, broth, soy sauce, pepper and five-spice powder. Re-cover. Microwave at High for 16 to 20 minutes, or until meat near bone is no longer pink and juices run clear, stirring twice to rearrange.

Using tongs, remove chicken from casserole. Cool slightly. Cut meat from bones. Discard bones. Set meat aside. Stir cornstarch mixture into hot broth. Microwave at High, uncovered, for 4 to 5 minutes, or until mixture is thickened and translucent, stirring every minute. Stir in mushrooms, chicken and vegetables. Cover. Set aside.

In small mixing bowl, combine baking mix and milk. Drop by spoonfuls onto chicken mixture. Sprinkle with sesame seed. Cover. Microwave at 70% (Medium High) for 8 to 10 minutes, or until dumplings are set and wooden pick inserted in center of each comes out clean, rotating casserole once.

*Defat broth by chilling 4 hours; skim and discard solidified fat from surface.

Per Serving: Calories: 418 • Protein: 42 g. • Carbohydrate: 37 g. • Fat: 11 g. • Cholesterol: 115 mg. • Sodium: 834 mg. Exchanges: 1¾ starch, 4¼ lean meat, 2 vegetable

Cranberry Roasted Chicken with Acorn Squash*

2 tablespoons sugar
1 tablespoon cornstarch
2 teaspoons grated orange peel, divided
1½ teaspoons ground cinnamon, divided
1¼ cups cranberry-apple juice, divided
1 cup halved fresh cranberries
1 teaspoon margarine or butter, melted
½ teaspoon ground ginger
5 to 7-lb. whole roaster chicken
1 orange, cut into 8 wedges
2 acorn squash (1½ lbs. each)

6 servings

In 4-cup measure, combine sugar, cornstarch, 1 teaspoon peel and ½ teaspoon cinnamon. Blend in 1 cup juice and the cranberries. Microwave at High for 4 to 5 minutes, or until glaze is thickened and translucent, stirring every minute. Set aside. In small bowl, combine margarine, remaining 1 teaspoon peel and 1 teaspoon cinnamon and the ginger. Rub mixture evenly over exterior and cavity of chicken. Stuff cavity with orange wedges. Secure legs together with string.

Place chicken breast-side-up in 10-inch square casserole. Heat conventional oven to 375°F. Microwave chicken at High for 20 minutes, rotating casserole once. Drain liquid from chicken in casserole. Immediately transfer casserole to conventional oven. Bake for 40 to 45 minutes, or until internal temperature in thickest portions of both thighs registers 185°F, basting with some of glaze during last 10 minutes of baking time. Place chicken on serving platter. Let stand for 10 minutes before carving.

Meanwhile, pierce each squash twice with fork. Microwave at High for 3 to 4 minutes, or until warm. (This will make them easier to cut.) Cut each squash into 6 wedges. Arrange wedges in 11 x 7-inch baking dish, cut-sides-up. Pour remaining ¼ cup juice over squash. Cover with plastic wrap. Microwave at High for 10 to 12 minutes, or until tender, rotating dish once. Let stand, covered, for 5 minutes. Brush with ½ cup glaze. Microwave at High for 2 minutes, or until hot. Serve squash and remaining glaze with chicken.

*Recipe not recommended for ovens with less than 600 cooking watts.

Per Serving: Calories: 669 • Protein: 58 g. • Carbohydrate: 36 g. • Fat: 32 g. • Cholesterol: 178 mg. • Sodium: 186 mg. Exchanges: 7½ lean meat, 2¾ vegetable, 1½ fruit, 2 fat

Chicken Marengo

1 tablespoon olive oil
3-lb. whole broiler-fryer
   chicken, cut into 8 pieces,
   skin removed
1 medium onion, thinly sliced
   and separated into rings
1 cup carrot strips (1½ ×
   ¼-inch strips)
2 tablespoons water
1 can (16 oz.) whole tomatoes,
   undrained and cut up
3 tablespoons tomato paste
1 tablespoon brandy
½ teaspoon sugar
½ teaspoon dried marjoram
   leaves
¼ teaspoon salt (optional)
¼ teaspoon garlic powder
⅛ teaspoon pepper

6 servings

In 12-inch nonstick skillet, heat oil conventionally over medium-high heat. Add chicken. Cook for 4 to 6 minutes, or just until brown on both sides. Remove from heat. Cover to keep warm. Set aside.

In 10-inch square casserole, combine onion, carrot strips and water. Cover. Microwave at High for 5 to 7 minutes, or until tender-crisp, stirring once. Drain. Stir in remaining ingredients. Re-cover. Microwave at High for 2 to 4 minutes, or until sauce is hot.

Arrange chicken over sauce with thickest portions toward outside. Spoon some of sauce over chicken. Cover. Microwave at High for 12 to 15 minutes, or until meat near bone is no longer pink and juices run clear, rearranging and turning chicken over once. To serve, spoon sauce over chicken. Serve with hot cooked rice and garnish with snipped fresh parsley, if desired.

Per Serving: Calories: 186 • Protein: 25 g.
• Carbohydrate: 8 g. • Fat: 6 g.
• Cholesterol: 76 mg. • Sodium: 369 mg.
Exchanges: 3 lean meat, 1½ vegetable

Chicken Schnitzel ▲

1⅓	cups apple juice	1	medium red or green cooking apple, cored and cut into 20 wedges
2	tablespoons thinly sliced green onion		
1	tablespoon packed brown sugar	2	boneless whole chicken breasts (8 to 10 oz. each), split in half, skin removed
2	teaspoons white vinegar		
1½	teaspoons grated lemon peel	¼	cup all-purpose flour
		1	egg white, beaten with 1 tablespoon skim milk
⅛	teaspoon white pepper		
1	tablespoon plus ½ teaspoon cornstarch mixed with 2 tablespoons water	½	cup unseasoned dry bread crumbs
		2	tablespoons vegetable oil

4 servings

In 4-cup measure, combine juice, onion, sugar, vinegar, peel and pepper. Microwave at High for 4 to 5 minutes, or until mixture is hot, stirring once. Stir in cornstarch mixture. Microwave at High for 1½ to 2 minutes, or until sauce is thickened and translucent, stirring every 30 seconds. Stir in apple wedges. Cover with plastic wrap. Set aside.

Place chicken between 2 sheets of plastic wrap. Gently pound to ¼-inch thickness with flat side of meat mallet. Place flour, egg white mixture and crumbs in 3 separate shallow dishes. Dredge chicken first in flour, then dip in egg mixture and then dredge in bread crumbs to coat. In 12-inch nonstick skillet, heat oil conventionally over medium-high heat. Cook chicken for 3 to 5 minutes, or just until brown on both sides and meat is no longer pink. Microwave sauce at High for 1½ to 2 minutes, or until hot, stirring once. To serve, spoon sauce over chicken.

Per Serving: Calories: 499 • Protein: 55 g. • Carbohydrate: 36 g. • Fat: 14 g.
• Cholesterol: 141 mg. • Sodium: 234 mg.
Exchanges: 1¼ starch, 6 lean meat, 1¼ fruit

Basque Drumsticks

8	chicken drumsticks (4 oz. each), skin removed
½	cup dry white wine
¼	cup white vinegar
3	tablespoons packed brown sugar
2	tablespoons olive oil
1	cup pitted dried prunes
1	jar (2½ oz.) pimiento-stuffed green olives, rinsed and drained
¼	cup finely chopped onion
2	tablespoons capers, drained
2	tablespoons dried basil leaves
2	tablespoons snipped fresh parsley
2	cloves garlic, minced
¼	teaspoon freshly ground pepper
2	bay leaves
¼	cup canned roasted red peppers, drained and chopped (optional)

4 servings

In 10-inch square casserole, arrange drumsticks with thickest portions toward outside. Set aside.

In medium mixing bowl, combine wine, vinegar, sugar and oil. Add remaining ingredients, except roasted red peppers. Mix well. Pour mixture over drumsticks, turning to coat. Cover. Chill 4 hours or overnight, turning drumsticks over once or twice.

Microwave at High, covered, for 20 to 24 minutes, or until meat near bone is no longer pink and juices run clear, rearranging and turning drumsticks over once. Sprinkle roasted red peppers evenly over drumsticks. Cover. Let stand for 5 minutes before serving.

Per Serving: Calories: 378 • Protein: 27 g.
• Carbohydrate: 40 g. • Fat: 14 g.
• Cholesterol: 94 mg. • Sodium: 652 mg.
Exchanges: 3½ lean meat, 2⅔ fruit

Chicken Cordon Bleu

- 2 boneless whole chicken breasts (8 to 10 oz. each), split in half, skin removed
- 1/4 cup shredded reduced-fat Swiss cheese (5 g. fat per oz.)
- 4 slices fully cooked lean ham (4$\frac{1}{2}$ × 4$\frac{1}{2}$ × $\frac{1}{8}$-inch)
- 1 tablespoon margarine or butter, melted
- 1/3 cup cornflake crumbs or unseasoned dry bread crumbs
- 1 teaspoon salt-free herb and spice blend

4 servings

Per Serving: Calories: 208 • Protein: 31 g.
• Carbohydrate: 1 g. • Fat: 8 g.
• Cholesterol: 83 mg. • Sodium: 277 mg.
Exchanges: 3 lean meat

Idea: Serve Chicken Cordon Bleu on toasted lettuce-lined kaiser rolls.

How to Make Chicken Cordon Bleu

Cut each breast half horizontally to create pocket. Place 1 tablespoon cheese on half of each ham slice. Fold over other half to enclose.

Insert 1 stuffed ham slice, folded-side-out, into each pocket. Set chicken aside.

Place margarine in small bowl. Combine crumbs and herb and spice blend in shallow dish. Brush chicken first with margarine, then dredge in crumb mixture to coat.

Arrange chicken on roasting rack. Microwave at High for 6 to 8 minutes, or until meat is no longer pink and juices run clear, rotating rack once.

Chicken with Mole Sauce

- 1 tablespoon olive oil
- 2 boneless whole chicken breasts (8 to 10 oz. each), split in half, skin removed
- 2 teaspoons cornstarch
- 2 teaspoons unsweetened cocoa
- 2 teaspoons packed brown sugar
- 1/4 teaspoon ground cinnamon
- 1/4 teaspoon crushed anise seed
- 1/8 teaspoon ground coriander
- 1/8 teaspoon cayenne
- 1 can (8 oz.) tomato sauce
- 1/4 cup low-sodium ready-to-serve chicken broth, defatted*
- 1/3 cup sliced green onions

4 servings

In 12-inch nonstick skillet, heat oil conventionally over medium-high heat. Add chicken. Cook for 4 to 6 minutes, or just until brown on both sides. Remove from heat. Set aside.

In 4-cup measure, combine cornstarch, cocoa, sugar, cinnamon, anise, coriander and cayenne. Blend in tomato sauce and broth. Microwave at High for 3 to 4 minutes, or until sauce is slightly thickened, stirring once.

In 10-inch square casserole, arrange chicken with thickest portions toward outside. Pour sauce over chicken. Cover. Microwave at High for 10 to 12 minutes, or until meat is no longer pink and juices run clear, rearranging and turning chicken over once. Sprinkle with onions. Re-cover. Microwave at High for 2 to 3 minutes, or until onions are tender-crisp.

*Defat broth by chilling 4 hours; skim and discard solidified fat from surface.

Per Serving: Calories: 202 • Protein: 26 g.
• Carbohydrate: 9 g. • Fat: 7 g.
• Cholesterol: 69 mg. • Sodium: 409 mg.
Exchanges: 3 lean meat, 1 1/2 vegetable

Chicken & Pasta Pilaf ▲

- 2 tablespoons margarine or butter
- 1 cup uncooked instant white rice
- 1/2 cup uncooked broken vermicelli (2-inch lengths)
- 1 can (14 1/2 oz.) diced tomatoes, undrained
- 1 1/4 cups hot water
- 1/2 cup chopped onion
- 1/2 cup chopped green pepper
- 1/2 cup raisins
- 1/4 cup sliced carrot
- 1/4 teaspoon ground cinnamon
- 1/4 teaspoon salt (optional)
- 1/4 teaspoon pepper
- 1 bay leaf
- 8 boneless skinless chicken thighs (2 to 3 oz. each), cut into 1/2-inch strips
- 1/4 cup slivered almonds, toasted
- 1/4 cup snipped fresh parsley

4 servings

In 10-inch square casserole, microwave margarine at High for 45 seconds to 1 minute, or until melted. Add rice and vermicelli. Stir to coat. Microwave at High for 4 to 5 minutes, or until vermicelli is lightly browned, stirring after first 2 minutes, and then after every minute.

Stir in tomatoes, water, onion, green pepper, raisins, carrot and seasonings. Cover. Microwave at High for 12 to 18 minutes, or until liquid is almost absorbed, stirring once. Stir in chicken. Re-cover. Microwave at High for 5 to 7 minutes, or until meat is no longer pink, stirring once. Stir in almonds and parsley. Remove and discard bay leaf.

Per Serving: Calories: 503 • Protein: 35 g. • Carbohydrate: 55 g. • Fat: 16 g.
• Cholesterol: 118 mg. • Sodium: 502 mg.
Exchanges: 2 starch, 3 1/2 lean meat, 2 vegetable, 1 fruit, 1 fat

Dijon Chicken au Gratin

Marinade:

   1 cup beer
   2 tablespoons vegetable oil
   2 tablespoons Dijon mustard
   1 tablespoon sugar
   1/4 teaspoon salt (optional)
   1/8 teaspoon white pepper

   2 boneless whole chicken breasts (8 to 10 oz.
     each), split in half, skin removed, cut into
     1/2-inch strips
1 1/2 lbs. red potatoes, peeled, cut into 3/4-inch
     cubes (4 cups)
   1 medium onion, thinly sliced
   2 tablespoons water
   1 medium red pepper, cut into thin strips
   3 tablespoons all-purpose flour
   1 cup skim milk
   1/2 cup beer
   1 cup shredded reduced-fat Cheddar cheese
     (5 g. fat per oz.)
   1/3 cup snipped fresh parsley
   1 tablespoon Dijon mustard
   1/2 cup cornflake crumbs
   2 tablespoons margarine, melted

6 servings

In medium mixing bowl, combine marinade ingredients. Add chicken. Stir to coat. Cover with plastic wrap. Chill at least 2 hours, stirring once or twice.

In 3-quart casserole, combine potatoes, onion and water. Cover. Microwave at High for 12 to 16 minutes, or until potatoes are tender, stirring every 4 minutes. Drain. Stir in red pepper strips. Cover. Set aside. Place flour in 4-cup measure. Blend in milk and beer. Microwave at High for 4 to 5 1/2 minutes, or until mixture thickens and bubbles, stirring every minute. Stir in cheese until melted. Stir in parsley and mustard. Pour cheese sauce over potato mixture. Stir to coat. Cover. Set aside.

In small mixing bowl, combine cornflake crumbs and margarine. Set aside. Drain and discard marinade from chicken. Blot chicken with paper towel to remove excess marinade. Heat 12-inch nonstick skillet conventionally over medium-high heat. Add chicken. Cook for 4 to 6 minutes, or just until brown on both sides. Stir into potato mixture. Sprinkle crumb mixture evenly over top. Microwave at High for 4 to 6 minutes, or until hot and bubbly around edges, rotating casserole once.

Per Serving: Calories: 368 • Protein: 27 g. • Carbohydrate: 36 g.
• Fat: 11 g. • Cholesterol: 61 mg. • Sodium: 480 mg.
Exchanges: 2 starch, 2 1/2 lean meat, 1/2 vegetable, 1/4 skim milk

Saucy Chicken Jambalaya

1 tablespoon vegetable oil
3 - lb. whole broiler-fryer chicken, cut into 8 pieces, skin removed
1 can (14½ oz.) diced tomatoes, undrained
1 cup water
½ cup chopped green pepper
½ cup chopped onion
3 tablespoons tomato paste
2 teaspoons chili powder
1 teaspoon sugar
½ teaspoon dried oregano leaves
¼ teaspoon salt (optional)
¼ teaspoon ground cumin
¼ teaspoon pepper
⅛ to ¼ teaspoon cayenne
1 cup frozen corn
¾ cup uncooked instant white rice

4 to 6 servings

In 12-inch nonstick skillet, heat oil conventionally over medium-high heat. Add chicken. Cook for 4 to 6 minutes, or just until brown on both sides. Remove from heat. Set aside. In 10-inch square casserole, combine remaining ingredients, except corn and rice. Cover. Microwave at High for 10 to 12 minutes, or until vegetables are tender-crisp, stirring once. Stir in corn and rice.

Arrange chicken over rice mixture with thickest portions toward outside. Cover. Microwave at High for 10 to 12 minutes, or until meat near bone is no longer pink, juices run clear and rice is tender, rearranging and turning chicken over once.

Per Serving: Calories: 253 • Protein: 26 g.
• Carbohydrate: 23 g. • Fat: 6 g.
• Cholesterol: 76 mg. • Sodium: 361 mg.
Exchanges: 1 starch, 3 lean meat, 1½ vegetable

Mostaccioli alla Puttanesca ▲

8 oz. uncooked mostaccioli
1 lb. ground chicken, crumbled
½ cup chopped onion
1 clove garlic, minced
1 teaspoon dried oregano leaves
¼ teaspoon crushed red pepper flakes
1 can (14½ oz.) diced tomatoes, drained

3 oz. fresh mushrooms, sliced (¾ cup)
¼ cup snipped fresh parsley
2 tablespoons capers, rinsed and drained
2 tablespoons tomato paste
1 tablespoon olive oil
½ teaspoon anchovy paste (optional)

4 servings

Prepare mostaccioli as directed on package. Rinse with hot water. Drain. Set aside. In 2-quart casserole, combine chicken, onion, garlic, oregano and red pepper flakes. Cover with wax paper or microwave cooking paper. Microwave at High for 5 to 7 minutes, or until meat is no longer pink, stirring once or twice to break apart. Drain.

Stir in remaining ingredients. Cover. Microwave at High for 2 to 4 minutes, or until hot, stirring once. Stir in mostaccioli. Microwave at High, uncovered, for 1 to 2 minutes, or until hot. Sprinkle with shredded fresh Parmesan cheese before serving, if desired.

Per Serving: Calories: 459 • Protein: 29 g. • Carbohydrate: 52 g. • Fat: 15 g.
• Cholesterol: 94 mg. • Sodium: 441 mg.
Exchanges: 3 starch, 3 lean meat, 1½ vegetable

Chicken Divan

  2 boneless whole chicken breasts (8 to 10 oz. each), split in half, skin removed, cut into ½-inch strips
  1 tablespoon white wine Worcestershire sauce
  2 teaspoons vegetable oil
1½ cups sliced fresh asparagus (1-inch lengths)
  ¼ cup finely chopped onion
  1 tablespoon water
  1 tablespoon margarine or butter
  1 tablespoon all-purpose flour
  1 teaspoon snipped fresh parsley
  ½ teaspoon grated lemon peel
  ½ teaspoon prepared mustard
  ¼ teaspoon low-sodium instant chicken bouillon granules
      Dash white pepper
  ¾ cup evaporated skim milk
  2 tablespoons shredded reduced-fat Swiss cheese (5 g. fat per oz.)
  1 tablespoon shredded fresh Parmesan cheese
  4 slices whole wheat bread, toasted

4 servings

In medium mixing bowl, combine chicken, Worcestershire sauce and oil. Stir to coat. Heat 12-inch nonstick skillet conventionally over medium-high heat. Add chicken. Cook for 3 to 6 minutes, or just until brown on both sides. Cover to keep warm. Set aside.

Meanwhile, in 1-quart casserole, combine asparagus, onion and water. Cover. Microwave at High for 5 to 6 minutes, or until vegetables are tender, stirring once. Drain. Cover to keep warm. Set aside.

In 2-cup measure, microwave margarine at High for 45 seconds to 1 minute, or until melted. Stir in flour, parsley, peel, mustard, bouillon and pepper. Blend in milk. Microwave at 50% (Medium) for 3 to 5 minutes, or until mixture thickens and bubbles, stirring every minute. Stir in cheeses until melted.

Arrange chicken evenly on toast. Top evenly with vegetable mixture and sauce.

Per Serving: Calories: 320 • Protein: 35 g. • Carbohydrate: 21 g. • Fat: 10 g. • Cholesterol: 77 mg. • Sodium: 371 mg.
Exchanges: 1 starch, 3¼ lean meat, 1 vegetable, ⅓ skim milk

Wild Rice Stuffed Roaster with Port Wine Gravy*

2¼ cups hot water, divided
 1 can (14½ oz.) low-sodium ready-to-serve
    chicken broth, defatted**
½ cup tawny port wine
½ cup uncooked wild rice
½ cup thinly sliced celery
¼ cup thinly sliced carrot
¼ cup chopped shallots or sliced green onions
 1 tablespoon vegetable oil
¼ cup coarsely chopped water chestnuts
 1 jar (2 oz.) sliced mushrooms, rinsed and
    drained
 2 cups corn bread stuffing mix
½ teaspoon seasoned salt

½ teaspoon pepper
 5 to 7-lb. whole roaster chicken
 1 tablespoon plus 1 teaspoon cornstarch
    mixed with 1 tablespoon tawny port wine

6 servings

*Recipe not recommended for ovens with less
than 600 cooking watts.
**Defat broth by chilling 4 hours; skim and dis-
card solidified fat from surface.

Per Serving: Calories: 740 • Protein: 62 g. • Carbohydrate: 40 g.
• Fat: 35 g. • Cholesterol: 178 mg. • Sodium: 648 mg.
Exchanges: 2¼ starch, 7½ lean meat, 1½ vegetable, 2 fat

How to Make Wild Rice Stuffed Roaster with Port Wine Gravy

Combine 1½ cups water, the broth, port and rice in 2-quart saucepan. Cook conventionally over medium-high heat until boiling. Cover. Reduce heat to low.

Cook for 45 to 50 minutes, or until kernels are open. Drain liquid from rice, reserving 1 cup. Set rice and reserved liquid aside.

Combine celery, carrot, shallots and oil in 10-inch square casserole. Microwave at High for 3 to 4 minutes, or until vegetables are tender-crisp, stirring once. Stir in remaining ¾ cup water, the water chestnuts and mushrooms. Cover.

Microwave at High for 2 to 3 minutes, or until mixture is very hot. Stir in rice and stuffing mix. Re-cover. Let stand for 5 minutes, or until stuffing is softened. Rub exterior and cavity of chicken evenly with seasoned salt and pepper.

Spoon stuffing mixture into cavity of chicken. Secure legs together with string. In same casserole, place chicken breast-side-up. Heat conventional oven to 375°F. Microwave chicken at High for 20 minutes, rotating casserole once.

Drain liquid from chicken in casserole. Immediately transfer casserole to conventional oven. Bake for 50 minutes to 1 hour, or until internal temperature in thickest portions of both thighs registers 185°F and internal temperature of stuffing registers 150°F.

Drain and discard drippings from chicken. Place chicken on serving platter. Let stand for 10 minutes before carving. Into same casserole, pour reserved rice liquid.

Stir with whisk to deglaze casserole. Microwave at High for 2 to 4 minutes, or until mixture is hot, stirring once with whisk. Using whisk, blend cornstarch mixture into hot mixture.

Microwave at High for 1½ to 2 minutes, or until gravy is thickened and translucent, stirring every 30 seconds. Serve gravy with chicken and stuffing.

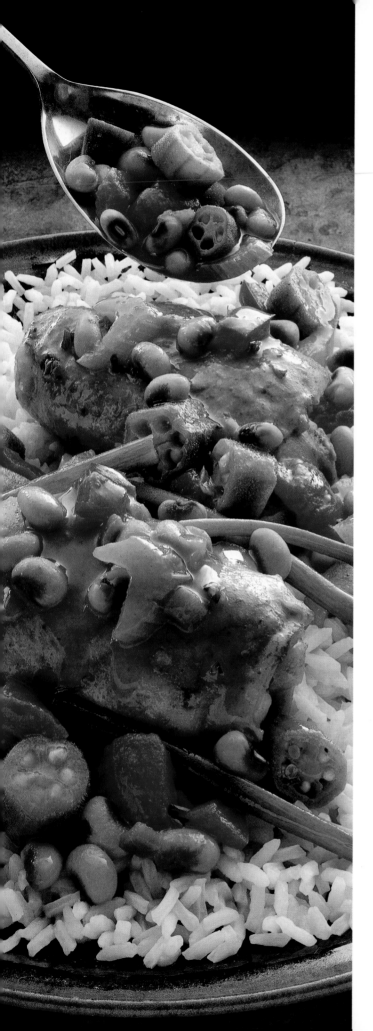

Chicken Gumbo

   ¼ cup all-purpose flour
   1 can (14½ oz.) low-sodium ready-to-serve
    chicken broth, defatted*, divided
   1 cup chopped red pepper
   ¾ cup sliced celery
   7 green onions, white portions sliced, green
    tops cut into 3-inch lengths and reserved
   2 cloves garlic, minced
   1 can (15 oz.) black-eyed peas, rinsed and
    drained
   1 can (14½ oz.) diced tomatoes, undrained
   1 can (4 oz.) chopped green chilies
   ¼ cup snipped fresh parsley
   ½ teaspoon pepper
   ½ teaspoon red pepper sauce
   8 bone-in chicken thighs (5 oz. each), skin
    removed
   ½ teaspoon Cajun seasoning
   1 pkg. (10 oz.) frozen cut okra, defrosted

6 servings

Heat conventional oven to 400°F. Sprinkle flour evenly into 8-inch square baking pan. Bake conventionally for 10 to 15 minutes, or until deep golden brown, stirring every 5 minutes. Set aside.

In 3-quart casserole, combine ¼ cup broth, the red pepper, celery, white portions of onions and the garlic. Cover. Microwave at High for 4 to 5 minutes, or until vegetables are tender-crisp, stirring once. Stir in flour. Blend in remaining broth, the peas, tomatoes, chilies, parsley, pepper and red pepper sauce.

Rub chicken with Cajun seasoning. Add to gumbo. Microwave at High for 25 to 35 minutes, or until meat near bone is no longer pink and juices run clear, stirring 2 or 3 times to rearrange. (If desired, remove chicken and cut meat from bones. Discard bones. Return meat to gumbo.)

Stir in reserved onion tops and the okra. Microwave at High for 2 to 4 minutes, or until onion tops are wilted and mixture thickens slightly, stirring once. Serve over hot cooked rice and sprinkle with filé powder, if desired. (Filé powder is a seasoning made from dried sassafras leaves, used to flavor and thicken Creole dishes.)

*Defat broth by chilling 4 hours; skim and discard solidified fat from surface.

Per Serving: Calories: 263 • Protein: 28 g. • Carbohydrate: 25 g.
• Fat: 5 g. • Cholesterol: 89 mg. • Sodium: 659 mg.
Exchanges: 1 starch, 3 lean meat, 1 vegetable

Zesty Chicken Scallopini

Sauce:

- 1 can (15 oz.) mangos, drained (reserve ¼ cup juice)
- ¼ cup low-sodium ready-to-serve chicken broth, defatted*
- ¼ cup diagonally sliced green onions (1-inch lengths)
- ¼ cup finely chopped red pepper
- ½ jalapeño pepper, seeded and finely chopped
- 1 clove garlic, minced
- ¼ teaspoon salt (optional)
- ¼ teaspoon freshly ground pepper
- 2 teaspoons cornstarch mixed with 1 tablespoon water

- 2 boneless whole chicken breasts (8 to 10 oz. each), split in half, skin removed
- 2 tablespoons all-purpose flour
- ¼ teaspoon salt (optional)
- ¼ teaspoon freshly ground pepper
- 1 tablespoon olive oil

4 servings

Cut mangos into ½-inch chunks. In 4-cup measure, combine mangos, reserved ¼ cup juice and remaining sauce ingredients, except cornstarch mixture. Microwave at High for 3 to 5 minutes, or until mixture is hot, stirring once. Stir in cornstarch mixture. Microwave at High for 1 to 1½ minutes, or until mixture is thickened and translucent, stirring every 30 seconds. Cover with plastic wrap to keep warm. Set aside.

Place chicken between 2 sheets of plastic wrap. Gently pound to ¼-inch thickness with flat side of meat mallet. In shallow dish, combine flour, salt and pepper. Dredge chicken in flour mixture to coat. In 12-inch nonstick skillet, heat oil conventionally over medium-high heat. Add chicken. Cook for 6 to 7 minutes, or just until brown on both sides and meat is no longer pink. To serve, spoon sauce over chicken. Serve with hot cooked rice or noodles, if desired.

*Defat broth by chilling 4 hours; skim and discard solidified fat from surface.

Per Serving: Calories: 251 • Protein: 27 g. • Carbohydrate: 21 g. • Fat: 6 g. • Cholesterol: 70 mg. • Sodium: 207 mg. Exchanges: ¼ starch, 3¼ lean meat, ½ vegetable, 1 fruit

91

Skillet Meals

Summer Vegetable Stir-fry

Skillet for the microwave oven is a 10-inch square Pyroceram™ casserole with a lid. Use it with a conventional stove top or oven, too. With some skillet meals, brown chicken conventionally in a 10 or 12-inch nonstick skillet before finishing it in the microwave oven with sauces, vegetables, rice or pasta. To bake breads conventionally, you may choose an old-fashioned cast-iron skillet.

Oriental Skillet Stir-fry

1 tablespoon sugar
2 teaspoons cornstarch
⅛ teaspoon cayenne
2 tablespoons soy sauce
1 tablespoon dry sherry
2 boneless whole chicken breasts (8 to 10 oz. each), split in half, skin removed, cut into thin strips
1 medium red pepper, cut into 1-inch chunks
1 medium red onion, sliced
8 oz. fresh snow pea pods

4 to 6 servings

In 10-inch square casserole, combine sugar, cornstarch and cayenne. Blend in soy sauce and sherry. Add chicken, red pepper and onion, stirring to coat. Cover. Microwave at High for 9 to 12 minutes, or until meat is no longer pink, stirring once or twice. Stir in pea pods. Re-cover. Microwave at High for 5 to 7 minutes, or until pea pods are tender-crisp, stirring once. Serve over hot cooked rice or fine egg noodles, if desired.

Per Serving: Calories: 134 • Protein: 19 g. • Carbohydrate: 9 g. • Fat: 2 g. • Cholesterol: 47 mg. • Sodium: 387 mg. Exchanges: 2 lean meat, 1½ vegetable

■ *Idea:* **Summer Vegetable Stir-fry:** Prepare
▲ as directed, except omit red pepper, onion
and pea pods. To cooked chicken, add 1½
cups each thinly sliced yellow summer squash
and zucchini, and ½ cup sliced green onions.
Cover. Microwave at High for 3 to 5 minutes,
or until vegetables are tender, stirring once.
Stir in 1 cup chopped seeded tomato. Serve
on bed of torn fresh spinach leaves. Garnish
with chopped radish, if desired.

■ *Idea:* **Peppered Pita Sandwich:** Prepare
▲ as directed, except increase cornstarch to
1 tablespoon and add ¼ teaspoon garlic
powder. Omit pea pods. Add 1 medium green
pepper, cut into thin strips. Cut red pepper
into thin strips. Microwave peppers with
chicken mixture as directed. Spoon into pita
bread halves. Top with hot yellow pepper
rings and shredded reduced-fat mozzarella
cheese, if desired.

■ *Idea:* **Oriental Stir-fry Salad:** Prepare as di-
▼ rected, except increase cornstarch to 1 tablespoon plus 1 teaspoon. Add 2 tablespoons
orange juice with soy sauce and sherry. Omit
onion and pea pods. Microwave chicken and
red pepper mixture as directed. Add 2 cups
shredded Chinese cabbage, 1 can (15 oz.)
baby corn cobs, rinsed and drained, and
1 can (11 oz.) mandarin orange segments,
drained. Toss to combine. Serve on lettuce-
lined plates or in baked tortilla shells.

■ *Idea:* **Spicy Satay Stir-fry:** Prepare as
▼ directed, except add ¼ teaspoon ground
ginger and increase cayenne to ¼ teaspoon.
Substitute 1 cup thin carrot strips for red pepper and onion. Omit pea pods. To cooked
chicken, add ¼ cup creamy peanut butter,
1 cup chopped red apple and ½ cup sliced
green onions. Microwave at High for 2 to 4
minutes, or until mixture is hot, stirring once.
Garnish with chopped peanuts, if desired.

Home-style Skillet Meals

Home-style Seasoning Mix

1 tablespoon margarine or
   butter, melted
½ teaspoon poultry seasoning

¼ teaspoon seasoned salt
¼ teaspoon pepper

Combine all ingredients. Use in recipes as directed.

Skillet à la King

2 boneless whole chicken
   breasts (8 to 10 oz. each),
   split in half, skin removed
   Home-style Seasoning Mix,
   above

Puff Pancake:
4 eggs
⅔ cup milk
⅓ cup all-purpose flour
¼ teaspoon salt

¼ cup plus 1 tablespoon
   margarine or butter, divided

¼ cup sliced green onions
¼ cup finely chopped red
   pepper
¼ cup finely chopped green
   pepper
1 pkg. (0.87 oz.) white sauce
   mix
¼ teaspoon dry mustard
1 cup milk
2 teaspoons fresh lemon juice

4 servings

Rub chicken with seasoning mix. Set aside. Heat conventional oven
to 425°F. In medium mixing bowl, combine pancake ingredients.
Beat with whisk until mixture is smooth. Set batter aside.

Place 3 tablespoons margarine in 10½-inch cast-iron skillet or 10-
inch deep-dish pie plate. Place in oven for 1 to 2 minutes, or until margarine is melted. Pour batter into hot skillet. Bake for 15 to 17 minutes,
or until pancake is puffed and edges are golden brown.

Meanwhile, heat 12-inch nonstick skillet conventionally over medium-
high heat. Add chicken. Brown on both sides. Reduce heat to low
and cook for 10 to 15 minutes longer, or until meat is no longer pink
and juices run clear, turning once. Remove from heat. Set aside.

In 4-cup measure, combine remaining 2 tablespoons margarine,
the onions and red and green peppers. Microwave at High for 3 to
5 minutes, or until vegetables are tender, stirring once. Stir in white
sauce mix and mustard. Blend in milk. Microwave at High for 5 to 6
minutes, or until sauce thickens and bubbles, stirring 3 or 4 times.
Stir in juice. Arrange chicken inside puff pancake. Spoon half of
sauce over chicken. Serve pancake in wedges. Serve with remaining sauce.

Per Serving: Calories: 502 • Protein: 38 g. • Carbohydrate: 18 g. • Fat: 31 g.
• Cholesterol: 297 mg. • Sodium: 699 mg.
Exchanges: ¾ starch, 4 lean meat, ½ skim milk, 3¾ fat

Herbed Artichoke Chicken Casserole

Home-style Seasoning Mix, page 96
2 boneless whole chicken breasts (8 to 10 oz. each), split in half, skin removed, cut into ½-inch strips
1 jar (6½ oz.) marinated artichoke hearts, drained (reserve marinade)
1 can (14½ oz.) ready-to-serve chicken broth
1 cup water
8 oz. uncooked medium egg noodles
⅓ cup snipped fresh parsley
1 jar (2 oz.) diced pimiento, drained

4 servings

In shallow dish, combine seasoning mix and chicken. Toss to coat. Set aside.

Cut each artichoke heart in half lengthwise. Set artichokes aside. In 10-inch square casserole, combine reserved artichoke marinade, broth and water. Cover. Microwave at High for 8 to 9 minutes, or until boiling. Stir in noodles and parsley. Re-cover. Microwave at High for 4 to 6 minutes, or until noodles are tender, stirring once. Set aside. (Small amount of liquid remaining in casserole will be absorbed during standing.)

Heat 12-inch nonstick skillet conventionally over medium-high heat. Add chicken. Cook for 3 to 6 minutes, or just until brown on both sides. Remove from heat. Add chicken, artichokes and pimiento to noodle mixture. Mix well. Cover. Microwave at High for 1 to 2 minutes, or until hot.

Per Serving: Calories: 440 • Protein: 36 g.
• Carbohydrate: 46 g. • Fat: 12 g.
• Cholesterol: 124 mg. • Sodium: 870 mg.
Exchanges: 2⅔ starch, 3 lean meat, 1 vegetable, ¾ fat

Chicken Skillet O'Brien ▲

1 lb. ground chicken, crumbled
½ cup sliced green onions
Home-style Seasoning Mix, page 96
2 cups frozen loose-pack cubed hash browns

1 cup frozen corn
¼ cup water
1 medium zucchini, sliced (1 cup)
1 cup chopped seeded tomato

4 servings

In 10-inch square casserole, combine chicken and onions. Microwave at High for 5 to 9 minutes, or until meat is no longer pink, stirring once or twice to break apart. Drain.

Add seasoning mix, hash browns, corn and water. Mix well. Cover. Microwave at High for 6 to 9 minutes, or until vegetables are tender, stirring once. Stir in zucchini. Microwave, uncovered, for 4 to 5 minutes, or until zucchini is tender-crisp, stirring once. Stir in tomato. Microwave at High for 2 to 3 minutes, or until hot.

Per Serving: Calories: 341 • Protein: 24 g. • Carbohydrate: 31 g. • Fat: 14 g.
• Cholesterol: 92 mg. • Sodium: 232 mg.
Exchanges: 2 vegetable, ⅓ fruit, 1 fat

Home-style Chicken Cassoulet

1/4 teaspoon dried thyme
   leaves
   Home-style Seasoning Mix,
   page 96
3-lb. whole broiler-fryer
   chicken, cut into 8 pieces,
   skin removed
2 slices bacon, chopped
1/2 cup chopped green pepper
1/2 cup chopped carrot
1/2 cup chopped onion
1 can (16 oz.) Great Northern
   beans, rinsed and drained
1 can (8 oz.) whole tomatoes,
   undrained and cut up
1 tablespoon packed brown
   sugar
1 tablespoon molasses
1/4 teaspoon salt
2 tablespoons margarine or
   butter
1/2 cup unseasoned dry bread
   crumbs
1/4 cup snipped fresh parsley

6 servings

Add thyme leaves to seasoning mix. Rub chicken with half of mixture. Set aside. Heat conventional oven to 425°F.

In 10-inch square casserole, microwave bacon at High for 2 to 3 minutes, or until brown and crisp, stirring once. Stir in green pepper, carrot and onion. Microwave at High for 3 to 4 minutes, or until vegetables are tender-crisp, stirring once. Stir in beans, tomatoes, sugar, molasses, salt and remaining seasoning mixture.

Arrange chicken over bean mixture with thickest portions toward outside. Cover. Microwave at High for 20 to 23 minutes, or until meat near bone is no longer pink and juices run clear, rearranging and turning chicken over once.

In small mixing bowl, microwave margarine at High for 45 seconds to 1 minute, or until melted. Stir in bread crumbs and parsley. Sprinkle mixture over chicken. Bake conventionally for 8 to 12 minutes, or until topping is deep golden brown.

Per Serving: Calories: 335 • Protein: 27 g. • Carbohydrate: 24 g. • Fat: 14 g.
• Cholesterol: 82 mg. • Sodium: 617 mg.
Exchanges: 1 starch, 3 lean meat, 1 vegetable, 1/3 fruit, 1 fat

Country Italian Skillet Meals

Country Italian Seasoning Mix

¼ cup finely chopped onion
1 tablespoon olive oil
1 clove garlic, minced

½ teaspoon Italian seasoning
¼ teaspoon seasoned salt
¼ teaspoon pepper

Combine all ingredients. Use in recipes as directed.

Italian Chicken

Country Italian Seasoning
  Mix, above
2 bone-in whole chicken
  breasts (10 to 12 oz. each),
  split in half, skin removed
1½ cups coarsely chopped
  green pepper
1 cup spaghetti sauce
1 can (14½ oz.) Roma
  tomatoes, drained and
  cut up
½ cup shredded Co-Jack
  cheese

4 servings

Heat 10-inch skillet conventionally over medium-high heat. Add seasoning mix. Cook for 30 seconds, or until onion is tender-crisp. Add chicken. Turn to coat. Cook for 4 to 6 minutes, or just until brown on both sides. Remove from heat. Set aside. Prepare rice, noodles or potatoes as directed below.

Sprinkle green pepper evenly over chicken. Microwave at High for 7 to 10 minutes, or until meat near bone is no longer pink and juices run clear (and potatoes are tender), rotating casserole once.

In small mixing bowl, combine spaghetti sauce and tomatoes. Spoon over chicken. Cover. Microwave at High for 3 to 4 minutes, or until hot. Sprinkle evenly with cheese. Re-cover. Let stand for 5 minutes, or until cheese is melted. Garnish with snipped parsley, if desired.

Per Serving: Calories: 325 • Protein: 32 g. • Carbohydrate: 18 g. • Fat: 14 g.
• Cholesterol: 83 mg. • Sodium: 697 mg.
Exchanges: 3½ lean meat, 3 vegetable, 1 fat

Idea: Italian Chicken with Rice: In 10-inch square casserole, combine 1¼ cups hot water and 1½ teaspoons margarine. Microwave at High for 4 to 5 minutes, or until boiling. Stir in 1½ cups uncooked instant white rice. Cover. Let stand for 5 minutes. Arrange chicken over rice with thickest portions toward outside. Continue as directed above.

Idea: Italian Chicken with Noodles: Toss 4 cups hot cooked medium egg noodles (8 oz. uncooked) with 1½ teaspoons margarine until margarine is melted. Spread evenly in 10-inch square casserole. Arrange chicken over noodles with thickest portions toward outside. Continue as directed above.

Idea: Italian Chicken with Potatoes: In 10-inch square casserole, combine 4 cups potato slices and ¼ cup water. Cover. Microwave at High for 10 minutes, stirring once. Drain. Arrange chicken over potatoes with thickest portions toward outside. Continue as directed above.

Chicken Lasagna Skillet

- 8 oz. uncooked mini lasagna noodles (4 cups)
  Country Italian Seasoning Mix, page 101
- 2 boneless whole chicken breasts (8 to 10 oz. each), split in half, skin removed, cut into ¾-inch pieces
- 1 jar (14 oz.) spaghetti sauce with mushrooms
- 1 cup ricotta cheese
- 1 cup shredded mozzarella cheese
- 2 tablespoons grated Parmesan cheese
- ¼ cup snipped fresh parsley

4 to 6 servings

Per Serving: Calories: 441 • Protein: 33 g.
• Carbohydrate: 42 g. • Fat: 15 g.
• Cholesterol: 73 mg. • Sodium: 491 mg.
Exchanges: 2 starch, 3½ lean meat, 2 vegetable, ¾ fat

How to Microwave Chicken Lasagna Skillet

Prepare noodles as directed on package. Rinse and drain. Set aside. In 10-inch square casserole, combine seasoning mix and chicken. Toss to coat. Cover. Microwave at High for 5 to 8 minutes, or until meat is no longer pink, stirring twice. Stir in noodles and spaghetti sauce. Cover.

Microwave at High for 6 to 8 minutes, or until mixture is hot, stirring once. In small mixing bowl, combine ricotta and mozzarella cheeses. Drop by tablespoonfuls over lasagna mixture. Sprinkle with Parmesan cheese and parsley. Cover. Microwave at High for 4 to 5 minutes, or until cheese is melted and mixture is hot.

Herbed Chicken with Orzo

6 oz. uncooked orzo pasta
   (1 cup)
   Country Italian Seasoning
   Mix, page 101
8 chicken drumsticks (4 oz.
   each), skin removed
¼ cup dry white wine
2 medium zucchini, cut
   lengthwise into quarters,
   then crosswise into 2-inch
   lengths
8 oz. fresh mushrooms, cut
   into quarters (2 cups)
1 medium red pepper, cut
   into 1-inch chunks

4 servings

Per Serving: Calories: 408 • Protein: 34 g.
• Carbohydrate: 45 g. • Fat: 9 g.
• Cholesterol: 94 mg. • Sodium: 195 mg.
Exchanges: 2½ starch, 3 lean meat,
1½ vegetable

How to Microwave Herbed Chicken with Orzo

Prepare orzo as directed on package. Rinse and drain. Set aside. In 10-inch square casserole, combine seasoning mix and drumsticks. Turn to coat. Arrange drumsticks with thickest portions toward outside. Cover. Microwave at High for 15 to 17 minutes, or until meat near bone is no longer pink and juices run clear, rearranging and turning over once.

Stir in wine. Add zucchini, mushrooms and red pepper. Re-cover. Microwave at High for 8 to 10 minutes, or until vegetables are tender-crisp, stirring once. Stir in orzo, or serve drumstick and vegetable mixture over orzo.

Mediterranean Skillet Meals

Mediterranean Seasoning Mix

2 teaspoons olive oil
2 cloves garlic, minced
½ teaspoon dried oregano
　 leaves
½ teaspoon grated lemon
　 peel

¼ teaspoon seasoned salt
¼ teaspoon freshly ground
　 pepper

Combine all ingredients. Use in recipes as directed.

Greek Chicken with Olives & Peppers

Mediterranean Seasoning
　 Mix, above
8 chicken drumsticks (4 oz.
　 each), skin removed
1 medium red or green
　 pepper, cut into 1-inch
　 chunks
1 medium onion, sliced
1 cup halved pitted black
　 olives

1 tablespoon olive oil
1½ cups chopped seeded
　 tomato
½ cup red wine
½ teaspoon dried thyme
　 leaves
¼ teaspoon pepper

4 servings

In shallow dish, combine seasoning mix and drumsticks. Turn to coat. Heat 10-inch nonstick skillet conventionally over medium-high heat. Add drumsticks. Cook for 4 to 6 minutes, or just until brown on both sides. Remove from heat. Set aside.

Meanwhile, in 10-inch square casserole, combine red pepper, onion, olives and oil. Cover. Microwave at High for 6 to 8 minutes, or until pepper and onion are tender-crisp, stirring once. Stir in tomato, wine, thyme and pepper. Re-cover. Microwave at High for 1½ to 2 minutes, or until hot.

Arrange drumsticks over vegetable mixture with thickest portions toward outside. Cover. Microwave at High for 9 to 11 minutes, or until meat near bone is no longer pink and juices run clear, rearranging and turning drumsticks over once.

Per Serving: Calories: 286 • Protein: 27 g. • Carbohydrate: 10 g. • Fat: 15 g.
• Cholesterol: 84 mg. • Sodium: 526 mg.
Exchanges: 3½ lean meat, 1 vegetable, ⅓ fruit, 1 fat

Lemon Chicken with Spinach Rice

1 cup coarsely chopped
   onions
1 tablespoon olive oil
2 cups torn fresh spinach
   leaves
1 pkg. (6¼ oz.) instant
   long-grain white and wild
   rice mix
2 cups water
2 tablespoons snipped fresh
   dill weed
¼ teaspoon salt
¼ teaspoon pepper
   Mediterranean Seasoning
   Mix, page 105
8 bone-in chicken thighs
   (5 oz. each), skin
   removed

4 servings

In 10-inch square casserole, combine onions and oil. Microwave at High for 4 to 6 minutes, or until onions are tender, stirring once. Stir in spinach. Microwave at High for 1½ to 2 minutes, or until mixture is hot and spinach is wilted. Discard seasoning packet from rice mix. Add rice, water, dill, salt and pepper to onion mixture. Mix well. Cover. Microwave at High for 8 to 10 minutes, or until rice is tender and liquid is almost absorbed. Let stand, covered, for 5 minutes, or until liquid is absorbed.

In shallow dish, combine seasoning mix and chicken. Turn to coat. Heat 10-inch nonstick skillet conventionally over medium-high heat. Add chicken. Cook for 4 to 6 minutes, or just until brown on both sides. Arrange chicken over rice mixture with thickest portions toward outside. Cover. Microwave at High for 8 to 10 minutes, or until meat near bone is no longer pink and juices run clear, rearranging and turning chicken over once. Before serving, sprinkle with fresh lemon juice and chopped fresh tomato, if desired.

Per Serving: Calories: 387 • Protein: 36 g. • Carbohydrate: 31 g. • Fat: 12 g. • Cholesterol: 134 mg. • Sodium: 375 mg.
Exchanges: 1¾ starch, 4 lean meat, 1 vegetable

◄ Curried Couscous & Chicken

   Mediterranean Seasoning
   Mix, page 105
2 boneless whole chicken
   breasts (8 to 10 oz. each),
   split in half, skin removed,
   cut into ½-inch strips
1½ cups hot water
2 tablespoons olive oil

1 tablespoon curry powder
¼ teaspoon salt
1 cup uncooked couscous
1 medium zucchini, cut in
   half lengthwise, then
   crosswise into slices
½ cup diagonally sliced
   green onions (1-inch
   lengths)

1 medium carrot, cut into
   2 x ¼-inch strips
⅓ cup chopped dates

4 servings

Per Serving: Calories: 454 • Protein: 33 g. • Carbohydrate: 52 g. • Fat: 13 g. • Cholesterol: 70 mg. • Sodium: 286 mg.
Exchanges: 2⅓ starch, 4 lean meat, 1 vegetable, ¾ fruit

How to Make Curried Couscous & Chicken

Combine seasoning mix and chicken in shallow dish. Toss to coat. Heat 10-inch nonstick skillet conventionally over medium-high heat. Add chicken. Cook for 3 to 4 minutes, or just until brown on both sides. Remove from heat. Set aside.

Combine water, oil, curry powder and salt in 10-inch square casserole. Cover. Microwave at High for 8 to 10 minutes, or until boiling. Stir in remaining ingredients, except chicken.

Cover. Let stand for 4 to 5 minutes, or until liquid is absorbed. Stir in chicken. Re-cover. Microwave at High for 3 to 4 minutes, or until mixture is hot, stirring once.

Southwest Skillet Meals

Southwest Seasoning Mix

2 teaspoons vegetable oil
½ teaspoon chili powder
¼ teaspoon ground cumin
¼ teaspoon seasoned salt
¼ teaspoon pepper

Combine all ingredients. Use in recipes as directed.

Chicken Enchilada Supper

  Southwest Seasoning Mix, above
8 chicken drumsticks (4 oz. each), skin removed
1 can (15 oz.) black beans, rinsed and drained
1 can (11 oz.) corn, rinsed and drained
½ cup picante sauce or salsa
⅓ cup chopped red pepper
⅓ cup sliced green onions
1 flour tortilla (10-inch)
2 teaspoons margarine or butter, melted

4 servings

Heat conventional oven to 400°F. In 10-inch square casserole, combine seasoning mix and drumsticks. Turn to coat. Arrange drumsticks with thickest portions toward outside. Cover. Microwave at High for 15 to 17 minutes, or until meat near bone is no longer pink and juices run clear, rearranging and turning drumsticks over once.

Stir in beans, corn, picante sauce, pepper and onions. Mix well. Microwave at High, uncovered, for 4 to 6 minutes, or until mixture is hot and peppers are tender-crisp, stirring once. Set aside.

Meanwhile, brush tortilla evenly with margarine. Cut into 1½ to 2-inch wedges. Place wedges on large baking sheet. Bake conventionally for 4 to 5 minutes, or until wedges are crisp and lightly browned. Garnish each serving with tortilla wedges.

Per Serving: Calories: 349 • Protein: 32 g. • Carbohydrate: 34 g. • Fat: 9 g. • Cholesterol: 94 mg. • Sodium: 838 mg.
Exchanges: 2 starch, 3 lean meat, 1 vegetable, ¾ fat

Fajita Stir-fry ▶

1 lb. ground chicken, crumbled
  Southwest Seasoning Mix, above
1 medium yellow summer squash, cut lengthwise into quarters, then crosswise into 2-inch lengths
1 small red onion, cut in half crosswise and sliced
½ medium red pepper, cut into 4 x ¼-inch strips
½ medium green pepper, cut into 4 x ¼-inch strips
1 or 2 jalapeño peppers, thinly sliced
4 flour tortillas (10-inch)

4 servings

In 10-inch square casserole, microwave chicken at High for 4 to 6 minutes, or until meat is no longer pink, stirring once or twice to break apart. Drain. Stir in seasoning mix. Add remaining ingredients, except tortillas. Cover. Microwave at High for 10 to 12 minutes, or until peppers are tender, stirring once. Spoon one-fourth of mixture down center of each tortilla. Top with salsa, shredded Cheddar cheese, guacamole or sour cream, if desired. Roll up.

Per Serving: Calories: 330 • Protein: 24 g. • Carbohydrate: 29 g. • Fat: 13 g. • Cholesterol: 92 mg. • Sodium: 382 mg.
Exchanges: 1½ starch, 3 lean meat, 1 vegetable, ¾ fat

Idea: Serve mixture over hot cooked rice, or toss with hot cooked fettucini.

Chicken Chili with Corn Bread

Corn Bread:

- 1 pkg. (7 oz.) corn muffin mix
- 1/4 teaspoon cayenne
- 1/4 teaspoon ground cumin
- 1/4 teaspoon coarsely ground black pepper
- 1 egg, beaten
- 1/4 cup milk
- 2 tablespoons margarine or butter, melted

Chili:

Southwest Seasoning Mix, page 108
- 2 boneless whole chicken breasts (8 to 10 oz. each), split in half, skin removed, cut into 3/4-inch pieces
- 1 can (16 oz.) chili beans in chili sauce
- 1 can (14 1/2 oz.) whole tomatoes, undrained and cut up
- 1/2 cup chopped green pepper
- 1/2 cup chopped onion
- 2 tablespoons tomato paste

4 to 6 servings

Heat conventional oven to 425°F. Grease 8-inch cast-iron skillet or 8-inch round cake pan. Set aside. In medium mixing bowl, combine corn bread ingredients. Mix just until dry ingredients are moistened. Heat prepared skillet in oven for 2 to 3 minutes. Spread batter in skillet. Bake for 10 to 12 minutes, or until golden brown and wooden pick inserted in center comes out clean. Set aside.

In 2-quart casserole, combine seasoning mix and chicken. Toss to coat. Cover. Microwave at High for 5 to 8 minutes, or until meat is no longer pink, stirring once. Stir in remaining chili ingredients. Re-cover. Microwave at High for 10 to 13 minutes, or until vegetables are tender-crisp, stirring once. Serve chili over corn bread wedges.

Per Serving: Calories: 377 • Protein: 26 g.
• Carbohydrate: 45 g. • Fat: 11 g.
• Cholesterol: 81 mg. • Sodium: 790 mg.
Exchanges: 2⅔ starch, 2 lean meat, 1 vegetable, ¾ fat

Cajun Chicken & Pasta

- 8 oz. uncooked rotini pasta (3 cups)
  Southwest Seasoning Mix, page 108
- 1/4 teaspoon dried thyme leaves
- 1/8 teaspoon cayenne
- 8 boneless skinless chicken thighs (2 to 3 oz. each), cut into 3/4-inch pieces
- 1 can (14 1/2 oz.) whole tomatoes, undrained and cut up
- 1 can (4 oz.) chopped green chilies
- 3 tablespoons tomato paste
- 1 medium green pepper, cut into 1-inch chunks
- 1/2 teaspoon sugar

4 servings

Prepare rotini as directed on package. Rinse and drain. Set aside. In 10-inch square casserole, combine seasoning mix, thyme and cayenne. Add chicken. Toss to coat. Cover. Microwave at High for 5 to 7 minutes, or until meat is no longer pink, stirring once. Stir in tomatoes, green chilies, tomato paste, green pepper and sugar. Mix well. Re-cover. Microwave at High for 7 to 9 minutes, or until green pepper is tender-crisp, stirring once. Stir in rotini. Re-cover. Microwave at High for 4 to 5 minutes, or until mixture is hot.

Per Serving: Calories: 470 • Protein: 41 g. • Carbohydrate: 53 g. • Fat: 10 g.
• Cholesterol: 134 mg. • Sodium: 659 mg.
Exchanges: 2¾ starch, 4 lean meat, 2 vegetable

Chicken Burrito Bake ▲

Southwest Seasoning Mix, page 108
2 boneless whole chicken breasts (8 to 10 oz. each), split in half, skin removed, cut into 3/4-inch pieces

Crust:
2 cups buttermilk baking mix
2 tablespoons yellow cornmeal

1/2 teaspoon chili powder
1/2 cup milk
1 egg

3/4 cup refried beans
1 avocado, sliced
1 jar (8 oz.) thick and chunky salsa, drained
1 cup shredded Cheddar cheese

4 to 6 servings

Heat conventional oven to 375°F. In 8-inch square baking dish, combine seasoning mix and chicken. Toss to coat. Cover with wax paper or microwave cooking paper. Microwave at High for 5 to 8 minutes, or until meat is no longer pink, stirring once. Drain. Set aside.

Wrap handle of 10-inch nonstick skillet with heavy-duty foil. In medium mixing bowl, combine baking mix, cornmeal and chili powder. Add remaining crust ingredients. Stir just until dry ingredients are moistened.

Spread batter over bottom and up sides of prepared skillet. Spread refried beans gently over batter in bottom of skillet. Top evenly with chicken, avocado slices, salsa and cheese. Bake for 25 to 30 minutes, or until crust is golden brown. Let stand for 5 minutes before cutting. Serve in wedges.

Per Serving: Calories: 455 • Protein: 29 g. • Carbohydrate: 39 g. • Fat: 20 g.
• Cholesterol: 105 mg. • Sodium: 1024 mg.
Exchanges: 2¼ starch, 3 lean meat, 1 vegetable, 2 fat

Idea: **Southwestern Chicken Pizza:** Prepare chicken as directed left. Set aside. Prepare crust as directed left, except spread batter over bottom and up sides of greased 12-inch pizza pan. Bake crust conventionally at 375°F for 6 to 8 minutes, or just until firm. Set aside. Omit remaining ingredients. In 10-inch square casserole, combine 1 cup thinly sliced zucchini, 1 cup thinly sliced red onion, 1 cup frozen corn with red and green peppers and 1 tablespoon olive oil. Toss to coat. Cover. Microwave at High for 5 to 6 minutes, or until mixture is hot, stirring once. Drain. Stir in chicken. Set aside. Spread one 8-oz. bottle taco sauce evenly over crust. Top evenly with chicken mixture. Sprinkle with 1/2 cup shredded Co-Jack cheese. Bake conventionally for 15 to 18 minutes, or until crust is golden brown and cheese is melted.

Garlic Herb Skillet Meals

Garlic Herb Seasoning Mix

2 teaspoons vegetable oil
2 cloves garlic, minced
½ teaspoon dried basil
    leaves or parsley flakes

¼ teaspoon seasoned salt
¼ teaspoon pepper

Combine all ingredients. Use in recipes as directed.

Honeyed Fig Chicken

1 pkg. (8 oz.) dried
    calimyrna figs, cut
    lengthwise into quarters
1 tablespoon orange zest
¾ cup fresh orange juice
⅓ cup fresh lemon juice
⅓ cup honey
2 tablespoons packed
    brown sugar
⅛ teaspoon cayenne
3 boneless whole chicken
    breasts (8 to 10 oz. each),
    split in half, skin removed
    Garlic Herb Seasoning
    Mix, above
1 cup chopped onions
½ cup sliced celery
1 tablespoon vegetable oil
2 cups hot water
1½ cups uncooked bulgur
    (cracked wheat)
1 tablespoon cornstarch
    mixed with 2 tablespoons
    water

6 servings

In small mixing bowl, combine figs, orange zest, juices, honey, sugar and cayenne. Cover with plastic wrap. Microwave at High for 2 to 3 minutes, or until mixture is hot, stirring once. Let stand for 5 minutes to plump figs. Rub chicken with seasoning mix. Heat 12-inch nonstick skillet conventionally over medium-high heat. Add chicken. Cook just until brown on both sides. Reduce heat to low. Pour fig mixture into skillet with chicken. Cover. Cook for 13 to 15 minutes, or until meat is no longer pink and juices run clear. Remove from heat. Set aside.

Meanwhile, in 10-inch square casserole, combine onions, celery and oil. Microwave at High for 4 to 6 minutes, or until vegetables are tender, stirring once. Stir in water. Cover. Microwave at High for 6 to 8 minutes, or until boiling. Stir in bulgur. Re-cover. Let stand for 8 to 10 minutes, or until water is absorbed.

Using slotted spoon, remove chicken from skillet. Arrange chicken over bulgur. Increase heat under skillet to medium. Stir cornstarch mixture into fig mixture. Heat 30 seconds to 1 minute, or until sauce is thickened and translucent, stirring constantly. Spoon over chicken and bulgur. Cover. Microwave at High for 2 to 3 minutes, or until hot. Garnish with additional orange zest, if desired.

Per Serving: Calories: 485 • Protein: 32 g. • Carbohydrate: 80 g. • Fat: 6 g.
• Cholesterol: 66 mg. • Sodium: 146 mg.
Exchanges: 1¾ starch, 4 lean meat, 3⅓ fruit

Chicken with Olives & Onions

    Garlic Herb Seasoning
      Mix, page 113
3 - lb. whole broiler-fryer
     chicken, cut into 8 pieces,
     skin removed
1 cup chopped onions
1 tablespoon olive oil
½ teaspoon dried parsley
     flakes
1½ cups uncooked instant
     brown rice
1¼ cups hot water
1 cup pimiento-stuffed
     green olives, rinsed and
     drained
½ cup dry sherry or ready-to-
     serve chicken broth

4 servings

Heat 12-inch nonstick skillet conventionally over medium-high heat. Add seasoning mix. Cook for 30 seconds. Add chicken. Turn to coat. Cook for 4 to 6 minutes, or just until brown on both sides. Remove from heat. Set aside.

In 10-inch square casserole, combine onions, oil and parsley. Cover. Microwave at High for 5 to 6 minutes, or until onions are tender, stirring once. Stir in rice, water, olives and sherry. Re-cover. Microwave at High for 5 to 6 minutes, or until boiling. Micro-wave at 50% (Medium) for 7 to 8 minutes longer, or until rice is tender and liquid is absorbed.

Arrange chicken over rice with thickest portions toward outside. Re-cover. Microwave at High for 8 to 12 minutes, or until meat near bone is no longer pink and juices run clear, rearranging and turning chicken over once.

Per Serving: Calories: 438 • Protein: 39 g.
• Carbohydrate: 36 g. • Fat: 16 g.
• Cholesterol: 114 mg. • Sodium: 1036 mg.
Exchanges: 2 starch, 4 lean meat,
½ vegetable, ¼ fruit, ¾ fat

Country French Chicken & Potato Stir-fry

Garlic Herb Seasoning Mix, page 113

- 2 boneless whole chicken breasts (8 to 10 oz. each), split in half, skin removed, cut into ¾-inch pieces
- 10 small new potatoes, thinly sliced (about 1 lb.)
- 1 pkg. (12 oz.) fresh whole baby carrots, each cut in half lengthwise
- 2 tablespoons water
- 2 teaspoons Worcestershire sauce
- ¼ teaspoon dried marjoram leaves
- 8 oz. fresh mushrooms, cut into quarters (2 cups)
- ½ cup sliced green onions

4 servings

In medium mixing bowl, combine seasoning mix and chicken. Toss to coat. Set aside.

In 10-inch square casserole, combine potatoes, carrots and water. Cover. Microwave at High for 9 to 13 minutes, or until vegetables are tender-crisp, stirring twice. Drain. Add chicken, Worcestershire sauce and marjoram. Mix well. Re-cover. Microwave at High for 7 to 11 minutes, or until meat is no longer pink and juices run clear, stirring once. Stir in mushrooms and onions. Re-cover. Microwave at High for 3 to 5 minutes, or until mixture is hot.

Per Serving: Calories: 296 • Protein: 31 g.
• Carbohydrate: 33 g. • Fat: 4 g.
• Cholesterol: 66 mg. • Sodium: 233 mg.
Exchanges: 1⅓ starch, 3 lean meat, 2 vegetable

Far East Skillet Meals

Far East Seasoning Mix

2 tablespoons soy sauce
2 tablespoons sliced green
   onion
1 tablespoon packed brown
   sugar

2 teaspoons vegetable oil
¼ teaspoon ground ginger
¼ teaspoon garlic powder

Combine all ingredients. Use in recipes as directed.

Polynesian Chicken

Far East Seasoning Mix, above
2 boneless whole chicken breasts (8 to 10 oz.
   each), split in half, skin removed, cut into
   ¾-inch pieces
1 can (20 oz.) pineapple chunks in juice,
   drained (reserve ⅔ cup juice for sauce)

Sauce:
1 tablespoon packed brown sugar
1 tablespoon cornstarch
¼ teaspoon ground ginger
¼ cup catsup
2 teaspoons white vinegar

1 medium red or green pepper, cut into
   1-inch chunks
1 small onion, cut into 12 wedges
1 can (14½ oz.) ready-to-serve chicken broth
1 cup uncooked long-grain white rice
⅓ cup water
¼ cup slivered almonds, toasted
¼ cup flaked coconut, toasted

4 servings

In shallow dish, combine seasoning mix and chicken. Toss to coat. Cover with plastic wrap. Chill at least ½ hour. In 4-cup measure, combine sugar, cornstarch and ginger. Blend in reserved juice and remaining sauce ingredients. Set pineapple chunks aside. Microwave at High for 2 to 3 minutes, or until sauce is thickened and translucent, stirring every minute. Cover. Set aside.

In 10-inch square casserole, combine chicken, red pepper and onion. Cover with wax paper or microwave cooking paper. Microwave at High for 8 to 9 minutes, or until meat is no longer pink, stirring once. Using slotted spoon, remove chicken mixture from casserole. Drain. Place mixture in medium mixing bowl. Cover. Set aside.

Wipe out casserole with paper towels. In same casserole, combine broth, rice and water. Cover. Microwave at High for 5 minutes. Microwave at 50% (Medium) for 20 to 25 minutes longer, or until rice is tender and liquid is absorbed. Add pineapple chunks and sauce to chicken mixture. Mix well. Spoon over rice. Microwave at High for 3 to 4 minutes, or until hot. Before serving, sprinkle evenly with almonds and coconut.

Per Serving: Calories: 563 • Protein: 34 g. • Carbohydrate: 79 g.
• Fat: 13 g. • Cholesterol: 70 mg. • Sodium: 1210 mg.
Exchanges: 2½ starch, 3 lean meat, ½ vegetable, 2½ fruit, ¾ fat

Far East Jeweled Chicken

Far East Seasoning Mix, page 116
2 boneless whole chicken breasts (8 to 10 oz. each), split in half, skin removed
½ cup dried apricots, cut in half
½ cup orange juice
½ cup orange marmalade
¼ cup chopped green pepper
2 tablespoons dry sherry, divided
¼ teaspoon paprika
¼ teaspoon salt
⅛ teaspoon white pepper
2 teaspoons cornstarch
½ cup halved seedless green grapes

4 servings

In shallow dish, combine seasoning mix and chicken. Turn to coat. Cover with plastic wrap. Chill 1 hour, turning once. In 4-cup measure, combine apricots, juice, marmalade, green pepper, 1 tablespoon sherry, the paprika, salt and pepper. Cover with plastic wrap. Microwave at High for 3 to 5 minutes, or until very hot. Let stand for 5 minutes to plump apricots.

In small bowl, combine remaining 1 tablespoon sherry and the cornstarch. Stir cornstarch mixture into apricot mixture. Microwave at High for 1 to 1½ minutes, or until mixture is thickened and translucent, stirring every 30 seconds. Stir in grapes. Cover. Set aside. Arrange chicken in 10-inch square casserole. Cover with wax paper or microwave cooking paper. Microwave at High for 4 to 9 minutes, or until meat is no longer pink and juices run clear, rearranging once. Drain. Top with fruit sauce. Serve over rice and sprinkle with toasted sliced almonds, if desired.

Per Serving: Calories: 357 • Protein: 27 g.
• Carbohydrate: 52 g. • Fat: 6 g.
• Cholesterol: 70 mg. • Sodium: 721 mg.
Exchanges: 3 lean meat, 3½ fruit

Saucy Oriental Chicken & Vegetables

Far East Seasoning Mix,
page 116
2 boneless whole chicken
breasts (8 to 10 oz. each),
split in half, skin removed
½ teaspoon grated orange
peel
¼ cup fresh orange juice
1 pkg. (9 oz.) frozen whole
baby carrots
1 pkg. (6 oz.) frozen snow
pea pods
1 tablespoon cornstarch
mixed with 2 tablespoons
water

4 servings

In 10-inch square casserole, combine seasoning mix and chicken.
Turn to coat. Cover. Microwave at High for 4 to 9 minutes, or until
meat is no longer pink and juices run clear, rearranging and turning
chicken over once. Stir in peel and juice. Add carrots and pea pods.
Cover. Microwave at High for 6 to 10 minutes, or until vegetables
are tender-crisp, stirring once.

Using slotted spoon, remove chicken and vegetables from casserole.
Add cornstarch mixture to liquid in casserole. Mix well. Microwave
at High for 3 to 5 minutes, or until sauce is thickened and translucent, stirring once or twice. Serve with chicken and vegetables.

Per Serving: Calories: 224 • Protein: 29 g. • Carbohydrate: 17 g. • Fat: 4 g.
• Cholesterol: 66 mg. • Sodium: 624 mg.
Exchanges: 3 lean meat, 3 vegetable

Meals for One & Two

Speedy Chicken Stir-fry

Seasoned Chicken Breast Fillet

1 pkg. (5 oz.) refrigerated boneless chicken breast fillet (country mustard and dill, lemon and herb,

teriyaki, mesquite barbecue, Italian-style blue cheese or Cajun)

1 serving

How to Microwave a Refrigerated Boneless Chicken Breast Fillet

Remove packaging and place fillet in 8-inch square baking dish. Cover with wax paper or microwave cooking paper.

Microwave at High for 4 to 6 minutes, or until meat is no longer pink and juices run clear, rotating dish once. Cool slightly. Use in recipes as directed right and opposite.

◄ *Idea:* **Spring Stir-fry Salad for Two:** Prepare 1 lemon and herb fillet as directed left. Cut into ¼-inch strips. Set aside. In 1½-quart casserole, microwave 1½ teaspoons margarine or butter at High for 30 to 45 seconds, or until melted. Add ½ cup cubed red potato (1-inch cubes). Cover. Microwave at High for 3 to 4 minutes, or until potato is tender, stirring once. Add ⅓ cup frozen whole baby carrots, ¼ cup frozen pearl onions, ¼ cup frozen peas and ⅛ teaspoon pepper. Microwave at High for 2 to 3 minutes, or until vegetables are tender. Stir in chicken. Serve on plates lined with Bibb lettuce.

Idea: **Country Chicken with Noodles for Two:** Prepare 1 mustard and dill fillet as directed left. Cut into 1-inch cubes. Place chicken in 1½-quart casserole. Add 2 cups hot cooked egg noodles, ¼ cup light sour cream, 1 tablespoon skim milk, ¼ teaspoon sugar and dash of pepper. Mix well. Microwave at High for 1 to 2 minutes, or until hot. Garnish with sprig of fresh dill, if desired.

◄ *Idea:* **Mesquite Barbecue Pita for One:** Prepare 1 mesquite barbecue fillet as directed left. Cut into ½-inch strips. Set aside. In 1-quart casserole, combine ½ cup green pepper strips, ¼ cup frozen corn, 2 tablespoons finely chopped red onion and 1 tablespoon water. Cover. Microwave at High for 3 to 4 minutes, or until vegetables are tender, stirring once. Drain. Add chicken. Spoon mixture evenly into 2 lettuce-lined pita halves. Garnish with tomato slices, if desired.

Idea: *Teriyaki Chicken with*
▶ **Ramen Noodles for One:**
Prepare 1 teriyaki fillet as
directed opposite. Cut into
1/2-inch strips. Set aside. Discard seasoning packet from
one 3-oz. package ramen
noodles. Prepare noodles as
directed on package. Drain.
In medium mixing bowl, toss
noodles with chicken, 1 tablespoon teriyaki sauce and
1/2 teaspoon sesame oil. In
1-quart casserole, combine
1/2 cup fresh snow pea pods,
6 red pepper strips, 1 tablespoon sliced green onion
and 2 teaspoons water. Cover.
Microwave at High for 1 to 2
minutes, or until tender-crisp.
Drain. Add to noodle mixture.
Toss to combine. Sprinkle
with additional sliced green
onion, if desired.

Idea: **Italian Chicken Pota-**
▶ **to Topper for Two:** Prepare
1 Italian-style blue cheese
fillet as directed opposite.
Cut into 1/2-inch cubes. Set
aside. In 1-quart casserole,
combine 1/2 cup fresh broccoli
flowerets and 2 teaspoons
water. Cover. Microwave at
High for 1 1/2 to 2 minutes, or
until broccoli is tender-crisp.
Drain. Add chicken. In 2-cup
measure, melt 1 tablespoon
margarine or butter at High
for 45 seconds to 1 minute.
Stir in 1 tablespoon all-
purpose flour, 1/8 teaspoon
salt and dash of pepper.
Blend in 1/2 cup milk. Microwave at High for 2 to 2 1/2 minutes, or until mixture thickens
and bubbles, stirring every
30 seconds. Pour over
chicken mixture. Mix well.
Spoon evenly over 2 split
hot baked potatoes.

Idea: **Cajun Chicken & Rice Salad for One:** Prepare 1 Cajun
fillet as directed opposite. Cut into 3/4-inch cubes. Set aside. In
1-quart casserole, combine 1/3 cup water and 1/4 cup uncooked instant brown rice. Cover. Microwave at High for 1 1/2 to 2 minutes,
or until water boils. Microwave at 50% (Medium) for 5 to 6 minutes longer, or until rice is tender and water is absorbed. Stir in
chicken, 2 tablespoons each finely chopped red and green pepper
and dash of cayenne. Cover and chill 2 hours, or until cold. Serve
on lettuce-lined plate. Garnish with sliced
green onion, if desired.

Tangy Chicken Kabobs

1 boneless whole chicken
    breast (8 to 10 oz.), split in
    half, skin removed
16 dried prunes
16 dried apricot halves
4 wooden skewers (10-inch)
2 tablespoons orange
    marmalade
2 tablespoons Catalina dressing

2 servings

Slice each breast half into six
½-inch strips. Thread chicken,
prunes and apricots evenly on
skewers. Arrange skewers on
roasting rack.

In small bowl, combine marmalade and dressing. Spoon
1 tablespoon mixture over each
kabob. Cover with wax paper
or microwave cooking paper.
Microwave at High for 4 to 6 minutes, or until meat is no longer
pink, rearranging and turning
kabobs over once. Serve with
rice pilaf, if desired.

Per Serving: Calories: 485 • Protein: 29 g.
• Carbohydrate: 77 g. • Fat: 9 g.
• Cholesterol: 70 mg. • Sodium: 249 mg.
Exchanges: 3 lean meat, 5 fruit

Italian-sauced Burgers ▲

½ lb. ground chicken,
    crumbled
¼ cup spaghetti sauce
2 tablespoons snipped fresh
    oregano
1 tablespoon shredded fresh
    Parmesan cheese
¼ teaspoon pepper
⅛ teaspoon garlic powder
⅛ teaspoon onion powder
2 hamburger buns, split
2 slices (1 oz. each)
    mozzarella cheese
1 tablespoon plus 1 teaspoon
    sliced black olives

2 servings

In medium mixing bowl, combine chicken, spaghetti sauce, oregano,
Parmesan cheese, pepper, garlic powder and onion powder. Shape
mixture into two 4-inch patties. Place on roasting rack. Cover with
wax paper or microwave cooking paper. Microwave at High for 6 to
7 minutes, or until meat is no longer pink, turning patties over and
rotating rack once. Place patties in lettuce-lined buns. Top each
with 1 slice mozzarella cheese and 2 teaspoons olives. Garnish with
parsley or serve with additional spaghetti sauce, if desired.

Per Serving: Calories: 433 • Protein: 31 g. • Carbohydrate: 28 g. • Fat: 21 g.
• Cholesterol: 28 mg. • Sodium: 661 mg.
Exchanges: 1½ starch, 3 lean meat, 1 vegetable, 2½ fat

Idea: **Single serving:** Wrap, label and freeze 1 cooked patty
no longer than 2 weeks. To defrost and heat, remove wrap. Place
patty on roasting rack. Microwave at 70% (Medium High) for 4 to
5 minutes, or until hot, turning over once.

Golden Chicken Noodle Soup

3 bone-in chicken thighs
  (5 oz. each), skin removed
2 cups cubed peeled sweet
  potato (1/2-inch cubes)
1 can (14½ oz.) ready-to-
  serve chicken broth
1/4 teaspoon ground ginger
1/8 teaspoon five-spice powder
1/8 teaspoon ground turmeric
2 oz. uncooked cellophane
  noodles
1/4 cup diagonally sliced
  green onions (1-inch
  lengths)

2 servings

In 2-quart casserole, combine chicken, sweet potato, broth, ginger, five-spice powder and turmeric. Cover. Microwave at High for 18 to 22 minutes, or until meat near bone is no longer pink and sweet potato is tender, turning chicken over and stirring mixture 2 or 3 times. Remove chicken. Cool slightly. Cut meat from bones. Discard bones. Return meat to casserole. Cover. Set aside.

Meanwhile, place noodles in small mixing bowl. Cover with hot water. Let stand for 10 minutes, or until softened. Drain. Cut noodles into 2-inch lengths. Stir into soup. Microwave at High for 1 to 2 minutes, or until hot, stirring once. Stir in onions. Serve immediately.

Per Serving: Calories: 413 • Protein: 29 g. • Carbohydrate: 59 g. • Fat: 6 g.
• Cholesterol: 101 mg. • Sodium: 1021 mg.
Exchanges: 3 starch, 3 lean meat, ½ vegetable

Herb & Spinach Stuffed Chicken Breasts

- 2 tablespoons chopped celery
- 2 tablespoons plus 1 teaspoon sliced green onion, divided
- 2 tablespoons margarine or butter, divided
- ½ cup crushed herb-seasoned stuffing mix
- ¼ cup frozen cut-leaf spinach, defrosted
- 2 boneless whole chicken breasts (8 to 10 oz. each), skin removed
- 1 tablespoon white wine
- ½ teaspoon grated lemon peel

2 servings

Per Serving: Calories: 458 • Protein: 54 g.
• Carbohydrate: 16 g. • Fat: 18 g.
• Cholesterol: 140 mg. • Sodium: 537 mg.
Exchanges: ¾ starch, 6 lean meat,
¾ vegetable

How to Make Herb & Spinach Stuffed Chicken Breasts

Combine celery, 2 tablespoons onion and 1 tablespoon margarine in small mixing bowl. Cover with plastic wrap. Microwave at High for 2 to 3 minutes, or until tender, stirring once.

Add stuffing and spinach. Mix well. Set aside. Place chicken between 2 sheets of plastic wrap. Gently pound to ⅛-inch thickness with flat side of meat mallet.

Spoon half of stuffing mixture on each chicken breast. Roll each breast around stuffing, tucking in ends and securing with wooden picks. Place on roasting rack.

Place remaining 1 tablespoon margarine in small bowl. Microwave at High for 45 seconds to 1 minute, or until melted. Add remaining 1 teaspoon onion, the wine and peel. Mix well.

Brush stuffed breasts with margarine mixture. Cover with wax paper or microwave cooking paper. Microwave at High for 5 to 6 minutes, or until meat is no longer pink and juices run clear, rotating rack once.

Let stand, covered, for 3 minutes. Slice each breast crosswise into six ½-inch slices. Serve with rice, if desired.

Cranberry Corn Bread Stuffed Chicken Breasts

2 tablespoons chopped celery
2 tablespoons chopped onion
1 teaspoon margarine or butter
½ cup corn bread stuffing mix
¼ cup whole-berry cranberry sauce, divided
2 tablespoons chili sauce, divided
2 boneless whole chicken breasts (8 to 10 oz. each), skin removed

2 servings

In small mixing bowl, combine celery, onion and margarine. Cover with plastic wrap. Microwave at High for 2 to 3 minutes, or until vegetables are tender, stirring once. Add stuffing, 3 tablespoons cranberry sauce and 1 tablespoon chili sauce. Mix well. Set aside.

Place chicken between 2 sheets of plastic wrap. Gently pound to ⅛-inch thickness with flat side of meat mallet. Spoon half of stuffing mixture on each chicken breast. Roll each breast around stuffing, tucking in ends and securing with wooden picks. Place on roasting rack.

In small bowl, combine remaining 1 tablespoon cranberry sauce and remaining 1 tablespoon chili sauce. Brush stuffed breasts with cranberry mixture. Cover with wax paper or microwave cooking paper. Microwave at High for 5 to 6 minutes, or until meat is no longer pink and juices run clear, rotating rack once. Let stand, covered, for 3 minutes. Slice each breast crosswise into six ½-inch slices.

Per Serving: Calories: 450 • Protein: 54 g.
• Carbohydrate: 36 g. • Fat: 9 g.
• Cholesterol: 140 mg. • Sodium: 638 mg.
Exchanges: ¾ starch, 6 lean meat, 1 fruit

Chicken & Black Bean Stuffed Peppers ▲

2 large green peppers (8 oz. each), cut in half lengthwise and seeded
2 tablespoons water
3 boneless skinless chicken thighs (2 to 3 oz. each), cut into ¼-inch strips
¼ cup chopped onion
¾ teaspoon chili powder
¼ teaspoon dried oregano leaves
⅛ teaspoon onion powder
⅛ teaspoon garlic powder
⅛ teaspoon ground cumin
1 can (16 oz.) black beans, rinsed and drained
¾ cup chopped seeded tomato
½ cup hot cooked white rice
¼ cup shredded Cheddar cheese

2 servings

Arrange pepper halves cut-side-up in 8-inch square baking dish. Sprinkle with water. Cover with plastic wrap. Microwave at High for 3 to 4 minutes, or until peppers are tender-crisp, rearranging once. Drain. Set aside.

In 2-quart casserole, combine chicken, onion, chili powder, oregano, onion powder, garlic powder and cumin. Cover with wax paper or microwave cooking paper. Microwave at High for 5 to 7 minutes, or until meat is no longer pink, stirring once. Drain. Add remaining ingredients, except cheese. Mix well. Spoon chicken mixture evenly into pepper halves. Cover with wax paper or microwave cooking paper. Microwave at High for 4 to 5 minutes, or until peppers are tender and chicken mixture is hot. Sprinkle evenly with cheese. Microwave at High for 1 to 2 minutes, or until cheese is melted.

Per Serving: Calories: 452 • Protein: 37 g. • Carbohydrate: 53 g. • Fat: 11 g.
• Cholesterol: 103 mg. • Sodium: 567 mg.
Exchanges: 2½ starch, 3 lean meat, 3 vegetable, ¼ fat

Eggplant Farci

3 boneless skinless chicken
    thighs (2 to 3 oz. each),
    cut into ¼-inch strips
1 tablespoon plus 1 teaspoon
    olive oil, divided
¼ teaspoon dried basil leaves
¼ teaspoon freshly ground
    pepper
⅛ teaspoon seasoned salt
⅛ teaspoon fennel seed,
    crushed
1 medium eggplant (1 lb.)
½ cup chopped seeded
    tomato
¼ cup thinly sliced zucchini,
    slices cut in half
¼ cup chopped onion
2 tablespoons dry sherry
1 tablespoon grated
    Parmesan cheese
½ teaspoon dried oregano
    leaves

2 servings

In 1-quart casserole, combine chicken, 1 teaspoon oil, the basil, pepper, salt and fennel. Cover with wax paper or microwave cooking paper. Microwave at High for 3 to 4 minutes, or until meat is no longer pink, stirring once. Drain. Set aside.

Cut eggplant in half lengthwise. Scoop out pulp, leaving ¼-inch-thick shells. Set shells aside. Coarsely chop pulp. In 2-quart casserole, combine pulp, remaining 1 tablespoon oil and remaining ingredients. Cover. Microwave at High for 7 to 9 minutes, or until vegetables are tender, stirring once. Drain. Stir in chicken.

Spoon mixture evenly into shells. Place stuffed shells on roasting rack. Cover with wax paper or microwave cooking paper. Microwave at High for 6 to 9 minutes, or until shells are tender, rotating and rearranging once. Top with plain yogurt, additional grated Parmesan cheese and snipped fresh parsley, if desired.

Per Serving: Calories: 321 • Protein: 25 g. • Carbohydrate: 21 g. • Fat: 14 g.
• Cholesterol: 90 mg. • Sodium: 231 mg.
Exchanges: 3 lean meat, 2½ vegetable, ½ fruit

Idea: Single serving: Wrap, label and freeze 1 cooked stuffed shell no longer than 2 weeks. To defrost and heat, remove wrap. Place shell on roasting rack. Microwave at 70% (Medium High) for 8 to 10 minutes, or until hot, rotating rack once.

Speedy Chicken Stir-fry

- 3 boneless skinless chicken breast tenders (1 oz. each)
- ½ teaspoon vegetable oil
- 1 cup cut-up fresh stir-fry vegetables
- 1½ teaspoons water
- 1 to 2 tablespoons prepared stir-fry or sweet-and-sour sauce

1 serving

In 1-quart casserole, combine chicken and oil. Cover with wax paper or microwave cooking paper. Microwave at High for 1½ to 2½ minutes, or until meat is no longer pink, stirring once. Drain. Place chicken in medium mixing bowl. Cover to keep warm. Set aside.

Wipe out casserole with paper towels. In same casserole, combine vegetables and water. Cover. Microwave at High for 2 to 3 minutes, or until tender-crisp, stirring once. Drain. Add to chicken. Stir in stir-fry sauce. Toss to coat. Serve over hot cooked rice or noodles, if desired.

Per Serving: Calories: 179 • Protein: 28 g. • Carbohydrate: 15 g. • Fat: 4 g. • Cholesterol: 49 mg. • Sodium: 171 mg.
Exchanges: 2 lean meat, 1½ vegetable, ½ fruit

■ *Idea:* **Speedy Chicken Stir-fry for Two:**
Double all ingredients. Prepare as directed, except substitute 1½-quart casserole for 1-quart casserole. Microwave chicken at High for 2½ to 3 minutes. Microwave vegetables at High for 3½ to 5 minutes.

Chicken Marsala ▼

- 8 oz. fresh green beans, broken into 2-inch lengths (2 cups)
- 1 cup sliced carrots
- ¼ cup water
- 1 tablespoon all-purpose flour
- ⅛ teaspoon salt
- ⅛ teaspoon pepper
- 1 boneless whole chicken breast (8 to 10 oz.), split in half, skin removed
- 1 tablespoon margarine or butter
- 1 tablespoon vegetable oil
- 8 oz. fresh mushrooms, sliced (2 cups)
- 1½ cups Marsala wine

2 servings

In 2-quart casserole, combine green beans, carrots and water. Cover. Microwave at High for 6 to 8 minutes, or until vegetables are tender-crisp, stirring once. Drain. Set aside.

In shallow dish, combine flour, salt and pepper. Dredge chicken in flour mixture to coat. In 12-inch nonstick skillet, heat margarine and oil conventionally over medium-high heat. Add chicken. Cook for 3 to 4 minutes, or just until brown on both sides. Add vegetables, mushrooms and Marsala. Cover. Reduce heat to medium. Cook for 8 to 10 minutes, or until meat is no longer pink, juices run clear and vegetables are tender.

Per Serving: Calories: 625 • Protein: 31 g. • Carbohydrate: 43 g. • Fat: 16 g. • Cholesterol: 70 mg. • Sodium: 313 mg.
Exchanges: 3 lean meat, 4½ vegetable, 1½ fruit, 6 fat

Chicken Breast with Mushroom-Basil Sauce

1 tablespoon plus 1½ teaspoons all-purpose flour, divided
⅛ teaspoon salt
⅛ teaspoon pepper
1 boneless whole chicken breast (8 to 10 oz.), split in half, skin removed
2 tablespoons margarine or butter, divided

8 oz. fresh mushrooms, sliced (2 cups)
¼ cup ready-to-serve chicken broth
2 tablespoons white wine
2 tablespoons to ¼ cup snipped fresh basil leaves
¼ cup milk

2 servings

In shallow dish, combine 1 tablespoon flour, the salt and pepper. Dredge chicken in flour mixture to coat. In 12-inch nonstick skillet, heat 1 tablespoon margarine conventionally over medium-high heat. Add chicken. Cook for 3 to 4 minutes, or just until brown on both sides. Remove from heat. Set aside.

In 1½-quart casserole, combine mushrooms and remaining 1 tablespoon margarine. Cover. Microwave at High for 6 to 10 minutes, or until mushrooms are tender. Drain. Set aside.

In 8-inch square baking dish, combine broth, wine and basil. Add chicken. Cover with wax paper or microwave cooking paper. Microwave at High for 5 to 7 minutes, or until meat is no longer pink and juices run clear, rotating dish once. Remove chicken from dish. Cover to keep warm. Set aside.

In 1-cup measure, combine remaining 1½ teaspoons flour and the milk. Blend milk mixture into liquid in baking dish. Microwave at High for 2 to 3 minutes, or until mixture thickens and bubbles, stirring every minute. Stir in mushrooms. Spoon sauce evenly over chicken.

Per Serving: Calories: 279 • Protein: 24 g. • Carbohydrate: 13 g. • Fat: 14 g.
• Cholesterol: 52 mg. • Sodium: 470 mg.
Exchanges: ½ starch, 2½ lean meat, 1 vegetable, 1½ fat

Idea: Serve over toasted English muffins or hot cooked noodles or rice.

◄ Chicken Provençal

1 tablespoon all-purpose flour
¼ teaspoon salt, divided
⅛ teaspoon pepper
1 boneless whole chicken breast (8 to 10 oz.), split in half, skin removed
1 tablespoon margarine or butter
1 tablespoon olive oil
½ cup chopped onion
1 clove garlic, minced
1 can (14½ oz.) diced tomatoes, undrained
1 cup red wine
½ teaspoon dried basil leaves
2 tablespoons chopped black olives
1 cup thinly sliced zucchini or yellow summer squash
¾ cup uncooked instant white rice
¾ cup ready-to-serve chicken broth

2 servings

In shallow dish, combine flour, ⅛ teaspoon salt and the pepper. Dredge chicken in flour mixture to coat. In 12-inch nonstick skillet, heat margarine and oil conventionally over medium-high heat. Add chicken, onion and garlic. Cook for 3 to 4 minutes, or just until chicken is brown on both sides. Add tomatoes, wine and basil. Mix well. Reduce heat to medium. Cover. Cook for 8 to 10 minutes, or until meat is no longer pink and juices run clear. Stir in olives.

Meanwhile, in 1½-quart casserole, combine zucchini, rice, broth and remaining ⅛ teaspoon salt. Cover. Microwave at High for 6 to 8 minutes, or until rice is tender and liquid is absorbed. Let stand, covered, for 3 minutes. Fluff with fork. Serve chicken with rice.

Per Serving: Calories: 571 • Protein: 34 g.
• Carbohydrate: 51 g. • Fat: 18 g.
• Cholesterol: 70 mg. • Sodium: 1338 mg.
Exchanges: 2 starch, 3 lean meat, 4 vegetable, 3 fat

Fresh Fennel Chicken with Orange Sauce

1 bone-in whole chicken breast (10 to 12 oz.), split in half, skin removed
1/4 teaspoon salt
1/4 teaspoon pepper
2 teaspoons vegetable oil
1 fresh fennel bulb, cut into 1/2-inch wedges (2 cups)

Sauce:

1/4 cup orange juice
1/4 cup chopped red pepper
2 tablespoons orange marmalade
1 teaspoon snipped fresh fennel leaf
1/8 teaspoon salt
Dash white pepper
1 teaspoon cornstarch mixed with 2 teaspoons water

2 servings

Sprinkle chicken evenly with salt and pepper. In 10-inch nonstick skillet, heat oil conventionally over medium-high heat. Add chicken. Cook for 4 to 6 minutes, or just until brown on both sides. Remove from heat.

Place fennel wedges in 2-quart casserole. Arrange chicken over fennel with thickest portions toward outside. Cover. Microwave at High for 6 to 8 minutes, or until meat near bone is no longer pink and juices run clear, rearranging and turning chicken over once. Drain. Cover to keep warm. Set aside.

In 2-cup measure, combine all sauce ingredients, except cornstarch mixture. Microwave at High for 1 1/2 to 2 minutes, or until mixture is hot and marmalade is melted. Stir in cornstarch mixture. Microwave at High for 30 seconds to 1 minute, or until sauce is thickened and translucent, stirring once. Spoon sauce over chicken.

Per Serving: Calories: 269 • Protein: 27 g. • Carbohydrate: 23 g. • Fat: 8 g.
• Cholesterol: 70 mg. • Sodium: 581 mg.
Exchanges: 3 lean meat, 1 1/2 vegetable, 1 fruit

Pollo en Corteza

1 boneless whole chicken
  breast (8 to 10 oz.), split in
  half, skin removed
¼ teaspoon garlic powder
1 pkg. (4 oz.) refrigerated
  crescent roll dough
¼ cup plus 2 tablespoons
  refried beans
2 tablespoons shredded
  Cheddar cheese
1 tablespoon plus 1 teaspoon
  salsa

2 servings

Per Serving: Calories: 420 • Protein: 33 g.
• Carbohydrate: 32 g. • Fat: 17 g.
• Cholesterol: 78 mg. • Sodium: 828 mg.
Exchanges: 2 starch, 3 lean meat,
¼ vegetable

Idea: **Single serving:** Cut
all ingredients in half. Prepare
chicken as directed, except
microwave for 3 to 4 minutes.

How to Make Pollo en Corteza

Heat conventional oven to
375°F. Place chicken in 8-inch
square baking dish. Sprinkle
evenly with garlic powder. Cover
with wax paper or microwave
cooking paper.

Microwave at High for 4 to 6
minutes, or until meat is no
longer pink and juices run
clear, rearranging once. Drain.
Set aside.

Remove crescent roll dough
from package. Separate into 2
rectangles. Press perforations
to seal. Press or roll each rectangle to 7 × 5-inch rectangle.

Combine beans, cheese and
salsa in small mixing bowl.
Spread each rectangle evenly
with bean mixture to within
1 inch of edge.

Place 1 chicken breast half in
center of each rectangle. Bring
long sides of dough together.
Pinch to seal. Pinch open edges
and corners to seal.

Place seam-side-down on
large baking sheet. Bake for
10 to 15 minutes, or until golden
brown. Top with sour cream,
guacamole and additional
salsa, if desired.

132

Chicken & Smoked Salmon Wellington

1 boneless whole chicken breast (8 to 10 oz.), split in half, skin removed
1 teaspoon grated lemon peel
1/8 teaspoon salt
1/8 teaspoon pepper
1 pkg. (4 oz.) refrigerated crescent roll dough
1/4 cup plus 2 tablespoons spreadable cream cheese with smoked salmon

2 servings

Heat conventional oven to 375°F. Place chicken in 8-inch square baking dish. Sprinkle evenly with peel, salt and pepper. Cover with wax paper or micro-wave cooking paper. Microwave at High for 4 to 6 minutes, or until meat is no longer pink and juices run clear, rearranging once. Drain. Set aside.

Remove crescent roll dough from package. Separate into 2 rectangles. Press perforations to seal. Press or roll each rect-angle to 7 × 5-inch rectangle. Spread each rectangle evenly with cream cheese to within 1 inch of edge.

Place 1 chicken breast half in center of each rectangle. Bring long sides of dough together. Pinch to seal. Pinch open edges and corners to seal. Place seam-side-down on large bak-ing sheet. Bake for 10 to 15 min-utes, or until golden brown. Garnish with lemon wedges, if desired.

Per Serving: Calories: 473 • Protein: 32 g.
• Carbohydrate: 24 g. • Fat: 27 g.
• Cholesterol: 108 mg. • Sodium: 932 mg.
Exchanges: 1½ starch, 3¾ lean meat, 3¼ fat

Gorgonzola Fettucini ▲

4 oz. uncooked spinach or egg fettucini
1 boneless whole chicken breast (8 to 10 oz.), split in half, skin removed
1/8 teaspoon garlic powder
1 tablespoon margarine or butter
1 tablespoon all-purpose flour
1/4 teaspoon freshly ground pepper
Dash ground nutmeg
3/4 cup skim milk
3 tablespoons crumbled Gorgonzola cheese, divided
1 tablespoon shredded fresh Parmesan cheese
1 tablespoon coarsely chopped hazelnuts, toasted
Snipped fresh parsley

2 servings

Prepare fettucini as directed on package. Rinse and drain. Place in medium mixing bowl. Cover to keep warm. Set aside.

Place chicken in 8-inch square baking dish. Sprinkle evenly with garlic powder. Cover with wax paper or microwave cooking paper. Microwave at High for 4 to 6 minutes, or until meat is no longer pink and juices run clear, rearranging once. Drain. Cool slightly. Cut into 3/4-inch pieces. Add to fettucini. Set aside.

In 2-cup measure, microwave margarine at High for 45 seconds to 1 minute, or until melted. Stir in flour, pepper and nutmeg. Blend in milk. Microwave at High for 2½ to 3½ minutes, or until sauce thick-ens and bubbles, stirring every minute. Add 2 tablespoons Gorgon-zola and the Parmesan cheese. Stir until cheeses are melted. Pour cheese sauce over pasta and chicken. Toss to coat. Place on serv-ing plates. Top evenly with remaining 1 tablespoon Gorgonzola, the hazelnuts and parsley.

Per Serving: Calories: 533 • Protein: 42 g. • Carbohydrate: 49 g. • Fat: 18 g.
• Cholesterol: 138 mg. • Sodium: 421 mg.
Exchanges: 1 starch, 3 lean meat, 3/4 vegetable, ½ fat

Curried Chicken & Vegetables

Veggie-Chicken Burgers ▲

- 1 lb. ground chicken, crumbled
- ½ cup shredded zucchini
- ½ cup shredded carrot
- 2 tablespoons unseasoned dry bread crumbs
- 1 teaspoon dried oregano leaves
- ¼ teaspoon celery seed
- ¼ teaspoon salt (optional)
- ¼ teaspoon pepper

4 servings

In medium mixing bowl, combine all ingredients. Shape mixture into four 4-inch round patties. Arrange patties on roasting rack. Cover with wax paper or microwave cooking paper. Microwave at High for 7 to 9 minutes, or until patties are firm and meat is no longer pink, turning patties over and rotating rack once. Serve in lettuce-lined whole wheat buns, if desired.

Per Serving: Calories: 197 • Protein: 21 g. • Carbohydrate: 5 g. • Fat: 10 g. • Cholesterol: 94 mg. • Sodium: 121 mg.
Exchanges: 3 lean meat, ½ vegetable, ¼ fat

Idea: **Veggie-Chicken Pizzas:** In 2-quart ▼ casserole, prepare meat mixture as directed, except omit bread crumbs and substitute fennel seed for celery seed. Cover with wax paper or microwave cooking paper. Microwave at High for 5 to 7 minutes, or until meat is no longer pink, stirring once or twice to break apart. Drain. Set aside. Heat conventional oven to 450°F. Remove and unroll dough from one 10-oz. pkg. refrigerated pizza crust dough. Cut dough into 6 equal portions, pressing each piece into 5-inch square. Place on greased baking sheet. Spread 1 tablespoon spaghetti sauce on center of each piece of dough. Top evenly with chicken mixture. Sprinkle pizzas evenly with ¼ cup finely chopped red pepper and ⅓ cup shredded reduced-fat mozzarella cheese. Bake conventionally for 14 to 16 minutes, or until crusts are golden brown.

Idea: **Veggie-Chicken Pasties:** In 2-quart
▲ casserole, prepare meat mixture as directed, except omit bread crumbs. Cover with wax paper or microwave cooking paper. Microwave at High for 5 to 7 minutes, or until meat is no longer pink, stirring once or twice to break apart. Drain. To chicken mixture, add 1½ cups cubed cooked red potatoes (½-inch cubes) and ⅓ cup light barbecue sauce. Mix well. Set aside. Heat conventional oven to 450°F. In medium mixing bowl, combine 2¼ cups light buttermilk baking mix and ¾ cup skim milk. Stir until soft dough forms. On lightly floured board, knead dough until no longer sticky. Divide into 6 equal portions. Roll each portion into 7-inch circle. Spoon ⅔ cup chicken mixture onto half of each circle. Fold opposite half over and press to seal. Place on greased baking sheet. Bake conventionally for 10 to 12 minutes, or until golden brown.

Idea: **Veggie-Chicken Meatballs:** In medium mixing bowl, prepare meat mixture as
▼ directed, except substitute snipped fresh dill weed for oregano. Shape mixture into 20 meatballs, about 1¼ inches in diameter. Arrange meatballs in single layer in 10-inch square casserole. Cover with wax paper or microwave cooking paper. Microwave at High for 6 to 8 minutes, or until meatballs are firm and no longer pink, rearranging once. Drain. Set aside. To ¼ cup melted light corn oil spread, add 1 tablespoon snipped fresh dill weed and 1 teaspoon grated lemon peel. Toss sauce with 3 cups hot cooked egg noodles. Serve meatballs over noodle mixture.

Chicken Polenta Pie

Polenta:

1½ cups water
½ cup yellow cornmeal
¼ teaspoon paprika
¼ teaspoon freshly ground pepper
¼ teaspoon salt (optional)

½ lb. ground chicken, crumbled
½ teaspoon dried summer savory
¼ teaspoon grated lemon peel
⅛ teaspoon freshly ground pepper
5 oz. fresh asparagus spears, cut into 1½-inch lengths (1 cup)
¼ cup finely chopped onion
1 tablespoon water
4 oz. fresh mushrooms, sliced (1 cup)
⅓ cup frozen cholesterol-free egg product, defrosted
⅓ cup skim milk
2 tablespoons all-purpose flour
1 medium tomato, thinly sliced

4 to 6 servings

Heat conventional oven to 350°F. In 4-cup measure, combine polenta ingredients. Microwave at High for 4 to 6 minutes, or until mixture is thickened and water is absorbed, stirring twice with whisk. Spray 9-inch pie plate with nonstick vegetable cooking spray. Pour polenta mixture into prepared pie plate. Spread evenly over bottom and up sides to form crust. Bake conventionally for 15 to 20 minutes, or until golden brown. Set aside.

In 1½-quart casserole, combine chicken, summer savory, peel and pepper. Cover with wax paper or microwave cooking paper. Microwave at High for 2 to 3 minutes, or until meat is no longer pink, stirring once or twice to break apart. Drain. Spoon mixture into crust.

Wipe out casserole with paper towels. In same casserole, combine asparagus, onion and water. Cover. Microwave at High for 4 to 5 minutes, or until vegetables are tender, stirring once. Drain. Spoon over chicken. Place mushrooms in same casserole. Cover. Microwave at High for 2 to 3 minutes, or until tender, stirring once. Drain. Spoon over asparagus.

In small mixing bowl, place egg product, milk and flour. Beat with whisk to combine. Pour mixture over filling in crust. Microwave pie at 50% (Medium) for 10 to 12 minutes, or until filling is set, rotating plate ¼ turn every 3 minutes. Garnish with tomato. Let stand for 5 minutes before serving.

Per Serving: Calories: 137 • Protein: 11 g. • Carbohydrate: 15 g. • Fat: 4 g.
• Cholesterol: 32 mg. • Sodium: 59 mg.
Exchanges: ¾ starch, 1 lean meat, ¾ vegetable

Ginger Chicken & Fresh Fruit Plate

3/4 lb. boneless skinless
    chicken breast tenders
2 tablespoons dry sherry
2 tablespoons reduced-
    sodium soy sauce
2 teaspoons grated fresh
    gingerroot
1 teaspoon sugar
1 clove garlic, minced

Dressing:

1 to 2 tablespoons Triple
    Sec liqueur or orange juice
2 teaspoons grated fresh
    gingerroot
1/2 teaspoon grated lemon
    peel
1 tablespoon fresh lemon
    juice

2 cups watermelon chunks
    (3/4-inch chunks)
1 1/2 cups cantaloupe melon
    balls
1 1/2 cups honeydew melon
    balls
    Red-tipped leaf lettuce
    Watermelon pickles
    (optional)

4 to 6 servings

Place chicken in 8-inch square baking dish. In small bowl, combine sherry, soy sauce, gingerroot, sugar and garlic. Pour over chicken, turning to coat. Cover with plastic wrap. Chill 30 minutes.

Remove plastic wrap from chicken. Re-cover with wax paper or microwave cooking paper. Microwave at High for 7 to 8 minutes, or until meat is no longer pink, stirring once. Drain. Cool slightly. Cover with plastic wrap. Chill at least 2 hours.

In small bowl, combine dressing ingredients. Set aside. In medium mixing bowl, combine fruit. Pour dressing over fruit. Toss to coat. Cover with plastic wrap. Chill at least 2 hours.

To serve, arrange lettuce leaves on large platter. Top with chicken and fruit. Garnish with watermelon pickles. Serve with warm muffins, bread sticks or sourdough bread slices, if desired.

Per Serving: Calories: 135 • Protein: 14 g.
• Carbohydrate: 15 g. • Fat: 1 g.
• Cholesterol: 33 mg. • Sodium: 246 mg.
Exchanges: 2 lean meat, 1 fruit

Chicken-Chili Crepes

Crepes:

- 3/4 cup plus 2 tablespoons all-purpose flour
- 2 tablespoons yellow cornmeal
- 1/2 teaspoon chili powder
- 1/4 teaspoon salt (optional)
- 1 1/2 cups skim milk
- 1/4 cup frozen cholesterol-free egg product, defrosted

Filling:

- 3/4 lb. boneless skinless chicken breast tenders
- 1 teaspoon vegetable oil
- 1/4 teaspoon ground cumin
- 1/4 teaspoon chili powder
- 1/4 teaspoon pepper
- 1/2 cup red pepper strips (2 × 1/4-inch strips)
- 1/2 cup sliced yellow summer squash
- 1/2 cup tomato sauce
- 1/3 cup sliced green onions

6 servings

In medium mixing bowl, combine crepes ingredients. Spray 6-inch nonstick skillet with nonstick vegetable cooking spray. Heat skillet conventionally over medium heat. Pour scant 1/4 cup batter into skillet. Lift and swirl skillet to coat bottom with batter. Cook for 3 to 4 1/2 minutes, or until crepe is set and golden brown, turning once. Repeat with remaining batter, spraying skillet with nonstick vegetable cooking spray after each crepe. Stack with wax paper between crepes. Set aside.

In 8-inch square baking dish, combine chicken, oil, cumin, chili powder and pepper. Cover with wax paper or microwave cooking paper. Microwave at High for 5 to 6 minutes, or until meat is no longer pink, stirring once. Drain. Stir in remaining ingredients. Microwave at High for 2 to 4 minutes, or until vegetables are tender-crisp, stirring once. Spoon chicken and vegetable mixture evenly down center of each crepe. Roll up crepes. Serve with salsa, if desired.

Per Serving: Calories: 185 • Protein: 19 g. • Carbohydrate: 22 g. • Fat: 2 g. • Cholesterol: 34 mg. • Sodium: 210 mg.
Exchanges: 1 starch, 1 1/2 lean meat, 1 vegetable, 1/4 skim milk

Idea: Before rolling up crepes, sprinkle lightly with shredded reduced-fat Cheddar cheese.

Chicken-stuffed Manicotti

 8 uncooked manicotti shells
 1 lb. ground chicken, crumbled
 ¼ cup finely chopped onion
 1 clove garlic, minced
 ¼ teaspoon freshly ground pepper
 1 can (8 oz.) no-salt-added whole tomatoes,
     drained and cut up
 ½ cup chopped seeded tomato
 ½ cup frozen broccoli flowerets, defrosted
 ⅔ cup light ricotta cheese (1 g. fat per oz.)
 ⅓ cup shredded reduced-fat mozzarella
     cheese (3 g. fat per oz.)
 1 egg white, beaten
 1 teaspoon dried oregano leaves
     Dash salt (optional)
 2 tablespoons light corn oil spread (8 g. fat
     per oz.)
 2 tablespoons all-purpose flour
 ⅛ teaspoon white pepper
 1 cup skim milk

4 to 6 servings

Heat conventional oven to 350°F. Prepare manicotti as directed on package. Rinse and drain. Set aside.

In 2-quart casserole, combine chicken, onion, garlic and pepper. Microwave at High for 6 to 8 minutes, or until meat is no longer pink, stirring once or twice to break apart. Drain. Add canned and fresh tomatoes, broccoli, cheeses, egg white, oregano and salt. Mix well. Stuff each shell with ½ cup chicken mixture. Arrange stuffed shells in single layer in 11 × 7-inch baking dish. Set aside.

In 2-cup measure, microwave corn oil spread at High for 45 seconds to 1 minute, or until melted. Stir in flour and white pepper. Blend in milk. Microwave at High for 2 to 3 minutes, or until sauce thickens and bubbles, stirring every minute. Pour sauce over stuffed shells. Cover with foil. Bake conventionally for 30 to 35 minutes, or until hot. Garnish with snipped fresh parsley or oregano, if desired.

Per Serving: Calories: 285 • Protein: 23 g. • Carbohydrate: 22 g.
• Fat: 11 g. • Cholesterol: 69 mg. • Sodium: 176 mg.
Exchanges: 1 starch, 3 lean meat, ¾ vegetable, ¼ skim milk

White Bean & Chicken Chili ▶

  2 boneless whole chicken breasts (8 to 10 oz. each), split in half, skin removed
1¾ teaspoons ground cumin, divided
  1 cup finely chopped green pepper
  1 cup chopped onions
  1 tablespoon light corn oil spread (8 g. fat per oz.)
  3 tablespoons all-purpose flour
  ½ cup water
  1 can (15 oz.) white kidney beans, rinsed and drained
  1 can (14½ oz.) low-sodium ready-to-serve chicken broth
  1 can (11 oz.) corn, rinsed and drained
  1 can (4 oz.) chopped green chilies
  2 tablespoons fresh lime juice
  ¼ teaspoon salt (optional)

6 servings

Place chicken in 8-inch square baking dish. Sprinkle evenly with ¼ teaspoon cumin. Cover with wax paper or microwave cooking paper. Microwave at High for 4 to 9 minutes, or until meat is no longer pink and juices run clear, rearranging once. Drain. Cool slightly. Cut into ¾-inch pieces. Set aside.

In 3-quart casserole, combine green pepper, onions and corn oil spread. Cover. Microwave at High for 4 to 6 minutes, or until vegetables are tender, stirring once. Stir in flour. Blend in water. Add chicken, remaining 1½ teaspoons cumin and remaining ingredients. Mix well. Microwave at High, uncovered, for 16 to 20 minutes, or until chili is slightly thickened, stirring 3 times. Top each serving with crushed tortilla chips, if desired.

Per Serving: Calories: 243 • Protein: 24 g.
• Carbohydrate: 27 g. • Fat: 5 g.
• Cholesterol: 47 mg. • Sodium: 416 mg.
Exchanges: 1½ starch, 2 lean meat,
1 vegetable

Chicken & Leek Soup ▲

  4 boneless skinless chicken thighs (2 to 3 oz. each), cut into ¾-inch pieces
  2 cups thinly sliced new potatoes
  1 cup thinly sliced leek
  ½ cup chopped carrot
  1 can (16 oz.) Great Northern beans, rinsed and drained
  1 can (14½ oz.) diced tomatoes, undrained
  1 can (14½ oz.) low-sodium ready-to-serve chicken broth
  ½ teaspoon dried basil leaves
  ½ teaspoon garlic powder
  ¼ teaspoon salt (optional)
  ¼ teaspoon pepper

4 servings

In 3-quart casserole, combine chicken, potatoes, leek and carrot. Cover. Microwave at High for 9 to 12 minutes, or until meat is no longer pink and vegetables are tender, stirring once or twice.

Stir in remaining ingredients. Re-cover. Microwave at High for 12 to 15 minutes, or until mixture boils, stirring once. Garnish each serving with grated Parmesan cheese, if desired.

Per Serving: Calories: 264 • Protein: 22 g. • Carbohydrate: 34 g. • Fat: 4 g.
• Cholesterol: 59 mg. • Sodium: 446 mg.
Exchanges: 1½ starch, 2 lean meat, 2 vegetable

Gazpacho Chicken ▲

2 boneless whole chicken breasts (8 to 10 oz. each), split in half, skin removed
1½ cups spicy vegetable juice, divided
⅛ teaspoon freshly ground pepper
1¾ cups no-salt-added vegetable juice
2 cups chopped seeded tomatoes
1 medium cucumber, thinly sliced
½ cup chopped green pepper
¼ cup sliced green onions
1 tablespoon fresh lemon juice
2 teaspoons vegetable oil
1 clove garlic, minced

6 servings

Place chicken in 8-inch square baking dish. Add ½ cup spicy vegetable juice and the pepper. Cover with wax paper or microwave cooking paper. Microwave at High for 8 to 11 minutes, or until meat is no longer pink and juices run clear, rearranging once. Drain. Cool slightly. Cut into ¾-inch pieces. Set aside.

In large mixing bowl, combine remaining 1 cup spicy vegetable juice and remaining ingredients. Add chicken. Mix well. Cover with plastic wrap. Chill at least 6 hours, or until cold. Top each serving with garlic-flavored croutons, if desired.

Per Serving: Calories: 158 • Protein: 19 g. • Carbohydrate: 12 g. • Fat: 4 g. • Cholesterol: 47 mg. • Sodium: 257 mg.
Exchanges: 2 lean meat, 2¼ vegetable

Meatball Cacciatore ▲

1 lb. ground chicken, crumbled	1 medium onion, sliced
1/4 cup unseasoned dry bread crumbs	1 can (14 1/2 oz.) diced tomatoes, undrained
1/2 teaspoon garlic powder	1 can (6 oz.) no-salt-added tomato paste
1/2 teaspoon Italian seasoning, divided	1/4 cup water
1/8 teaspoon pepper	1 teaspoon sugar
2 egg whites, beaten	2 cups sliced yellow summer squash
1 cup green pepper strips (2 × 1/4-inch strips)	

6 servings

In medium mixing bowl, combine chicken, bread crumbs, garlic powder, 1/4 teaspoon Italian seasoning, the pepper and egg whites. Shape mixture into 12 meatballs, about 1 1/2 inches in diameter. Set aside. In 10-inch square casserole, combine green pepper and onion. Cover. Microwave at High for 5 to 6 minutes, or until vegetables are tender-crisp, stirring once. Drain. Remove vegetables from casserole. Set aside.

In same casserole, arrange meatballs in single layer. Cover with wax paper or microwave cooking paper. Microwave at High for 6 to 7 minutes, or until meatballs are firm and no longer pink, rearranging once.

Stir in vegetable mixture, tomatoes, tomato paste, water, sugar and remaining 1/4 teaspoon Italian seasoning. Re-cover. Microwave at High for 5 to 7 minutes, or until mixture is hot. Stir in squash. Re-cover. Microwave at High for 2 to 3 minutes, or until squash is tender-crisp, stirring once. Serve over hot cooked pasta, if desired.

Per Serving: Calories: 197 • Protein: 17 g. • Carbohydrate: 16 g. • Fat: 7 g.
• Cholesterol: 63 mg. • Sodium: 243 mg.
Exchanges: 1/4 starch, 2 lean meat, 2 1/2 vegetable, 1/4 fat

Chicken Patty Melt with Apple-Pepper Relish

Relish:

1 small red cooking apple, cored and finely chopped (1/2 cup)
1/3 cup finely chopped red pepper
1/3 cup finely chopped green pepper
3 tablespoons finely chopped red onion
2 tablespoons frozen apple juice concentrate, defrosted
1 tablespoon finely chopped serrano chili pepper
1/4 teaspoon freshly ground pepper

1 lb. ground chicken, crumbled
2 tablespoons seasoned dry bread crumbs
1 egg white, beaten
2 tablespoons shredded reduced-fat Monterey Jack cheese (5 g. fat per oz.)

4 servings

In small mixing bowl, combine relish ingredients. Cover with plastic wrap. Set aside. In medium mixing bowl, combine chicken, bread crumbs and egg white. Shape mixture into four 4-inch round patties. Arrange patties on roasting rack. Cover with wax paper or microwave cooking paper. Microwave at High for 6 to 8 minutes, or until meat is no longer pink, turning patties over and rotating rack once.

Top patties with some of relish. Sprinkle evenly with cheese. Microwave at High, uncovered, for 1 to 2 minutes, or until cheese is melted. Serve in whole wheat buns, if desired. Top evenly with remaining relish.

Per Serving: Calories: 234 • Protein: 23 g.
• Carbohydrate: 10 g. • Fat: 11 g.
• Cholesterol: 97 mg. • Sodium: 231 mg.
Exchanges: 1/4 starch, 3 lean meat, 1/2 vegetable, 1/3 fruit, 1/4 fat

Polynesian Chicken Stew

2 boneless whole chicken breasts (8 to 10 oz. each), split in half, skin removed

2 tablespoons plus 1 teaspoon light corn oil spread (8 g. fat per oz.), divided

¼ teaspoon pepper, divided

3 cups cubed peeled sweet potatoes (1-inch cubes)

½ cup water

¾ cup green pepper strips (2 × ¼-inch strips)

1 can (8 oz.) pineapple chunks in juice, drained (reserve ½ cup juice)

¼ cup chopped onion

2 tablespoons all-purpose flour

1 cup low-sodium ready-to-serve chicken broth

2 kiwifruit, peeled and sliced Fresh coconut strips (optional)

4 servings

Place chicken in 8-inch square baking dish. Dot with 1 teaspoon corn oil spread. Sprinkle with ⅛ teaspoon pepper. Cover with wax paper or microwave cooking paper. Microwave at High for 4 to 9 minutes, or until meat is no longer pink and juices run clear, rearranging once. Drain. Cool slightly. Cut into ¾-inch pieces. Set aside. In 3-quart casserole, combine sweet potatoes and water. Cover. Microwave at High for 6 to 10 minutes, or until potatoes are tender, stirring once. Add pepper strips. Re-cover. Microwave at High for 3 to 5 minutes, or until pepper strips are tender, stirring once. Drain. Add chicken and pineapple chunks. Cover to keep warm. Set aside.

In 4-cup glass measure, combine onion and remaining 2 tablespoons corn oil spread. Microwave at High for 2 to 3 minutes, or until spread is melted and onion is tender. Stir in flour and remaining ⅛ teaspoon pepper. Blend in broth and reserved juice. Microwave at High for 6 to 8 minutes, or until sauce thickens and bubbles, stirring every minute. Pour sauce over chicken and vegetable mixture. Mix well. Cover. Microwave at High for 2 to 3 minutes, or until stew is hot. Spoon into individual serving bowls. Garnish with kiwifruit and fresh coconut.

Per Serving: Calories: 378 • Protein: 29 g. • Carbohydrate: 45 g. • Fat: 9 g. • Cholesterol: 70 mg. • Sodium: 132 mg.
Exchanges: 1½ starch, 3 lean meat, ½ vegetable, 1¼ fruit

Spring Lemon Chicken Platter

3 - lb. whole broiler-fryer
    chicken, cut into
    8 pieces, skin removed
1½ teaspoons grated lemon
    peel, divided
¼ cup fresh lemon juice,
    divided
⅛ teaspoon white pepper
12 small new potatoes (about
    1¼ lbs.)
1 cup plus 2 tablespoons
    water, divided
3 tablespoons light corn oil
    spread (8 g. fat per tbsp.)
1 tablespoon snipped fresh
    chives
1 lb. fresh asparagus spears
¼ cup sugar
1 tablespoon plus 2
    teaspoons cornstarch
1 to 2 drops yellow food
    coloring
    Fresh whole strawberries
    Lemon slices

6 servings

Arrange chicken in 10-inch square casserole with thickest portions toward outside. Sprinkle with 2 tablespoons juice, ½ teaspoon peel and the pepper. Cover. Microwave at High for 20 to 23 minutes, or until meat near bone is no longer pink and juices run clear, rearranging once. Drain. Cover to keep warm. Set aside.

Remove thin strip of peel from each potato. In 2-quart casserole, combine potatoes and 2 tablespoons water. Cover. Microwave at High for 8 to 10 minutes, or until potatoes are tender, stirring once. Drain. Add corn oil spread and chives. Toss to coat. Cover to keep warm. Set aside.

In 11 × 7-inch baking dish, arrange asparagus spears with tips toward center. Add ¼ cup water. Cover with plastic wrap. Microwave at High for 6½ to 9½ minutes, or until asparagus is tender, rearranging spears once. Drain. Cover to keep warm. Set aside.

In 4-cup measure, combine sugar and cornstarch. Blend in remaining ¾ cup water, 2 tablespoons juice and 1 teaspoon peel and the food coloring. Microwave at High for 4 to 7 minutes, or until sauce is thickened and translucent, stirring after every minute. Spoon over chicken and asparagus. Serve with potatoes. Garnish with strawberries and lemon slices.

Per Serving: Calories: 306 • Protein: 27 g. • Carbohydrate: 31 g. • Fat: 8 g.
• Cholesterol: 76 mg. • Sodium: 128 mg.
Exchanges: 1¼ starch, 3 lean meat, ¾ fruit

Chicken with Cucumber Dill Sauce & New Potatoes

Sauce:

⅓ cup coarsely chopped seeded cucumber

¼ cup reduced-calorie mayonnaise

¼ cup light sour cream

1 tablespoon snipped fresh dill weed

½ teaspoon grated lemon peel

½ teaspoon sugar
    Dash garlic salt

2 boneless whole chicken breasts (8 to 10 oz. each), split in half, skin removed

¼ teaspoon white pepper, divided

⅛ teaspoon paprika
    Dash salt (optional)

8 small new potatoes (about 12 oz.)

2 tablespoons water

1 tablespoon light corn oil spread (8 g. fat per tbsp.)

1 tablespoon snipped fresh dill weed

¼ teaspoon grated lemon peel

4 servings

In small mixing bowl, combine sauce ingredients. Cover with plastic wrap. Chill. Place chicken in 8-inch square baking dish. Sprinkle evenly with ⅛ teaspoon pepper, the paprika and salt. Cover with wax paper or microwave cooking paper. Microwave at High for 4 to 9 minutes, or until meat is no longer pink and juices run clear, rearranging once. Drain. Cover to keep warm. Set aside.

Remove thin strip of peel from each potato. In 1½-quart casserole, combine potatoes and water. Cover. Microwave at High for 5 to 8 minutes, or until potatoes are tender, stirring once. Drain. Add corn oil spread, dill weed, peel and remaining ⅛ teaspoon pepper. Toss to coat. Serve chicken with sauce and potatoes. Garnish with cucumber slices and sprigs of fresh dill, if desired.

Per Serving: Calories: 296 • Protein: 29 g. • Carbohydrate: 18 g.
• Fat: 11 g. • Cholesterol: 80 mg. • Sodium: 195 mg.
Exchanges: 2¾ starch, 4 lean meat,
½ skim milk, 1¼ fat

Spinach & Ricotta Stuffed Chicken

2 teaspoons paprika
½ teaspoon dried parsley flakes, crushed
½ teaspoon freshly ground pepper, divided
¼ teaspoon salt (optional)
3-lb. whole broiler-fryer chicken
½ cup finely chopped onion
8 cups torn fresh spinach leaves
½ cup light ricotta cheese (1 g. fat per oz.)
¼ cup shredded fresh Parmesan cheese
1 jar (2 oz.) sliced pimiento, drained
1 to 2 cloves garlic, minced
1 teaspoon dried basil leaves
½ teaspoon dried oregano leaves

4 to 6 servings

Per Serving: Calories: 300 • Protein: 34 g.
• Carbohydrate: 6 g. • Fat: 16 g.
• Cholesterol: 93 mg. • Sodium: 237 mg.
Exchanges: 4½ lean meat, 1 vegetable, ½ fat

How to Microwave Spinach & Ricotta Stuffed Chicken

Combine paprika, parsley, ¼ teaspoon pepper and the salt in small bowl. Rub outside of chicken evenly with mixture. Set aside.

Place onion in 3-quart casserole. Cover. Microwave at High for 2 to 4 minutes, or until tender, stirring once.

Stir in remaining ingredients. Cover. Microwave at High for 4 to 5 minutes, or just until spinach is wilted, stirring once. Spoon spinach mixture into cavity of chicken. Secure legs together with string. Place chicken breast-side-up on roasting rack.

Microwave at High for 21 to 28 minutes, or until internal temperature in thickest portions of both thighs registers 185°F and internal temperature of stuffing registers 150°F, rotating rack twice. Let stand for 10 minutes before carving.

Broiled Chicken Breasts with Spinach & Tomatoes ▶

- 2 bone-in whole chicken breasts (10 to 12 oz. each), split in half, skin removed
- 2 tablespoons fresh lemon juice
- 2 tablespoons light corn oil spread (8 g. fat per tbsp.)
- ¼ teaspoon salt (optional)
- ¼ teaspoon pepper
- ⅛ teaspoon paprika
- 8 cups torn fresh spinach leaves
- 1 cup halved cherry tomatoes
- ½ teaspoon lemon pepper seasoning

4 servings

Rub chicken evenly with juice. Place on rack in broiler pan. In small bowl, microwave corn oil spread at High for 45 seconds to 1 minute, or until melted. Add salt, pepper and paprika. Brush chicken with half of mixture.

Place chicken under conventional broiler, with surface of meat 6 inches from heat. Broil for 12 to 19 minutes, or until meat near bone is no longer pink and juices run clear, turning chicken over once and brushing with remaining corn oil spread mixture.

Place spinach in 3-quart casserole. Cover. Microwave at High for 5 to 7 minutes, or just until spinach is wilted, stirring once. Add tomatoes and seasoning. Cover. Let stand for 3 minutes. Arrange spinach mixture on serving platter. Top with chicken.

Per Serving: Calories: 209 • Protein: 29 g.
• Carbohydrate: 6 g. • Fat: 7 g.
• Cholesterol: 70 mg. • Sodium: 287 mg.
Exchanges: 3 lean meat, 1¼ vegetable

Sweet Barbecued Drumsticks

- 1 tablespoon light corn oil spread (8 g. fat per tbsp.)
- ⅓ cup no-salt-added tomato paste
- 3 tablespoons low-sodium catsup
- 3 tablespoons packed brown sugar
- 2 teaspoons lemon juice
- 1 teaspoon liquid smoke flavoring
- ¼ teaspoon freshly ground pepper
- ¼ teaspoon dry mustard
- ⅛ teaspoon garlic powder
- ⅛ teaspoon celery seed
- 6 chicken drumsticks (4 oz. each), skin removed

4 servings

In 2-cup measure, microwave corn oil spread at High for 45 seconds to 1 minute, or until melted. Add remaining ingredients, except drumsticks. Mix well. Arrange drumsticks on roasting rack with thickest portions toward outside. Brush one-third of sauce mixture over drumsticks. Cover with wax paper or microwave cooking paper. Microwave at High for 6 minutes.

Turn drumsticks over. Brush with one-third of sauce. Re-cover. Microwave at High for 5 to 6 minutes, or until meat near bone is no longer pink and juices run clear. Drain. Brush drumsticks with remaining sauce. Microwave at High for 1 to 2 minutes, or until hot.

Per Serving: Calories: 235 • Protein: 26 g. • Carbohydrate: 17 g. • Fat: 6 g.
• Cholesterol: 94 mg. • Sodium: 144 mg.
Exchanges: 3 lean meat, 2 vegetable, ½ fruit

Cranberry Chicken

1½ cups fresh cranberries
1 can (8 oz.) pineapple tidbits in juice, undrained
1 medium red cooking apple, cored and chopped (¾ cup)
¼ cup golden raisins
¼ cup sugar
¼ teaspoon ground cinnamon

¼ teaspoon ground allspice
2 tablespoons frozen apple juice concentrate, defrosted
3- lb. whole broiler-fryer chicken, cut into quarters, skin removed

4 servings

Per Serving: Calories: 335 • Protein: 33 g. • Carbohydrate: 41 g. • Fat: 5 g. • Cholesterol: 105 mg. • Sodium: 120 mg. Exchanges: 4 lean meat, 2½ fruit

How to Make Cranberry Chicken

Combine all ingredients, except chicken, in 2-quart casserole. Cover. Microwave at High for 10 to 13 minutes, or until berries just begin to split and sauce thickens slightly. Cover to keep warm. Set aside.

Spray 10-inch nonstick skillet with nonstick vegetable cooking spray. Heat conventionally over medium-high heat. Add chicken. Cook for 4 to 6 minutes, or just until brown on both sides.

Place chicken in 10-inch square casserole. Cover. Microwave at High for 9 to 11 minutes, or until meat near bone is no longer pink and juices run clear, rearranging once. Spoon sauce over chicken.

Chicken Paprikash

 2 bone-in whole chicken breasts (10 to 12 oz. each), split in half, skin removed
 1½ teaspoons paprika, divided
 ½ teaspoon onion powder
 ¼ teaspoon pepper
 ¼ cup low-sodium ready-to-serve chicken broth
 1 tablespoon all-purpose flour
 ¼ teaspoon salt (optional)
 1 cup evaporated skim milk
 1 pkg. (9 oz.) frozen cut green beans
 ½ teaspoon grated lemon peel
 2 tablespoons light sour cream

4 servings

Sprinkle chicken evenly with ½ teaspoon paprika, the onion powder and pepper. Spray 12-inch nonstick skillet with nonstick vegetable cooking spray. Heat skillet conventionally over medium-high heat. Add chicken. Cook for 4 to 6 minutes, or just until brown on both sides. Place in 10-inch square casserole. Pour broth over chicken. Cover. Microwave at High for 8 to 10 minutes, or until meat near bone is no longer pink and juices run clear, rearranging once. Drain. Cover to keep warm. Set aside.

In 4-cup measure, combine flour, remaining 1 teaspoon paprika and the salt. Blend in milk. Microwave at High for 3 to 5 minutes, or until mixture thickens and bubbles, stirring once or twice. Add beans and peel. Stir to break apart beans. Microwave at High for 3 to 5 minutes, or until beans are tender-crisp, stirring once. Stir in sour cream. Spoon sauce over chicken.

Per Serving: Calories: 233 • Protein: 33 g. • Carbohydrate: 15 g. • Fat: 4 g. • Cholesterol: 75 mg. • Sodium: 140 mg. Exchanges: 3 lean meat, 1½ vegetable, ½ skim milk

Honey Dijon Chicken ▲

 3- lb. whole broiler-fryer chicken, cut into 8 pieces, skin removed
 ½ teaspoon garlic powder
 ¼ teaspoon paprika
 ¼ cup white wine vinegar
 2 tablespoons honey
 2 tablespoons Dijon mustard
 2 teaspoons cornstarch
 ¼ cup snipped fresh chives

4 to 6 servings

Sprinkle chicken evenly with garlic powder and paprika. Spray 12-inch nonstick skillet with nonstick vegetable cooking spray. Heat conventionally over medium-high heat. Add chicken. Cook for 4 to 6 minutes, or just until brown on both sides. Arrange in 10-inch square casserole with thickest portions toward outside. Set aside.

In 2-cup measure, combine vinegar, honey, mustard and cornstarch. Microwave at High for 1½ to 2 minutes, or until sauce is thickened, stirring once. Spoon sauce over chicken. Cover. Microwave at High for 10 to 15 minutes, or until meat near bone is no longer pink and juices run clear, rearranging once. Sprinkle evenly with chives.

Per Serving: Calories: 166 • Protein: 23 g. • Carbohydrate: 8 g. • Fat: 4 g. • Cholesterol: 76 mg. • Sodium: 235 mg. Exchanges: 3 lean meat, ½ fruit

Poached Chicken & Pineapple Salsa ▲

- 2 boneless whole chicken breasts (8 to 10 oz. each), split in half, skin removed
- ¼ cup unsweetened pineapple juice
- 1 clove garlic, minced

Salsa:

- 1¼ cups shredded savoy cabbage
- 1 can (8 oz.) pineapple tidbits in juice, drained (reserve ½ cup juice for dressing)
- ½ cup shredded carrot
- ¼ cup finely chopped green pepper
- ¼ cup sliced green onions
- ¼ cup snipped fresh cilantro

Dressing:

- ½ cup reserved pineapple juice
- 2 tablespoons vegetable oil
- 1 clove garlic, minced

4 servings

Place chicken in 8-inch square baking dish. Pour juice over chicken. Sprinkle with garlic. Cover with wax paper or microwave cooking paper. Microwave at High for 8 to 11 minutes, or until meat is no longer pink and juices run clear, rearranging once. Cool slightly. Cover with plastic wrap. Chill at least 3 hours.

In large mixing bowl, combine salsa ingredients. In small bowl, combine dressing ingredients. Pour over salsa. Toss to coat. Cover with plastic wrap. Chill at least 3 hours. Drain and discard juice from chicken. Spoon salsa over chicken.

Per Serving: Calories: 257 • Protein: 27 g. • Carbohydrate: 15 g. • Fat: 10 g. • Cholesterol: 70 mg. • Sodium: 74 mg.
Exchanges: 3 lean meat, 1 vegetable, ¾ fruit

Curried Chicken & Vegetables

- 2 bone-in whole chicken breasts (10 to 12 oz. each), split in half, skin removed
- ¼ teaspoon seasoned salt
- ¼ teaspoon pepper
- 1 tablespoon vegetable oil
- 2 cups frozen broccoli, carrots, water chestnuts and red pepper
- 1 tablespoon water
- 1 teaspoon curry powder
- ¼ teaspoon ground cumin
- ¼ teaspoon fennel seed, crushed
- ⅛ teaspoon cayenne (optional)

4 servings

Sprinkle chicken evenly with seasoned salt and pepper. In 12-inch nonstick skillet, heat oil conventionally over medium-high heat. Add chicken. Cook for 4 to 6 minutes, or just until brown on both sides. Remove from heat.

Arrange chicken in 10-inch square casserole with thickest portions toward outside. Cover with wax paper or microwave cooking paper. Microwave at High for 7 to 10 minutes, or until meat near bone is no longer pink and juices run clear, rearranging and turning chicken over once. Drain. Arrange chicken on serving platter. Cover to keep warm. Set aside.

In same casserole, combine remaining ingredients. Cover. Microwave at High for 5 to 7 minutes, or until vegetables are tender-crisp, stirring once. Spoon vegetable mixture over chicken.

Per Serving: Calories: 226 • Protein: 29 g. • Carbohydrate: 12 g. • Fat: 7 g. • Cholesterol: 70 mg. • Sodium: 176 mg.
Exchanges: 3 lean meat, 2½ vegetable

Honey Cinnamon Chicken with Fruited Rice

1 cup uncooked converted white rice

2½ cups water

½ cup snipped mixed dried fruit

½ teaspoon ground cinnamon

2 bone-in whole chicken breasts (10 to 12 oz. each), split in half, skin removed

Glaze:

3 tablespoons honey

1 tablespoon light corn oil spread (8 g. fat per tbsp.)

2 teaspoons sugar

½ teaspoon ground cinnamon

4 servings

Per Serving: Calories: 434 • Protein: 29 g.
• Carbohydrate: 68 g. • Fat: 5 g.
• Cholesterol: 70 mg. • Sodium: 83 mg.
Exchanges: 2 starch, 3 lean meat, 2½ fruit

In 2-quart saucepan, combine rice, water, fruit and cinnamon. Cook conventionally over medium-high heat until mixture comes to a boil. Reduce heat to low. Cover. Cook for 20 minutes, or until rice is tender and liquid is absorbed. Cover to keep warm. Set aside.

Meanwhile, place chicken in 8-inch square baking dish. Cover with wax paper or microwave cooking paper. Microwave at High for 11 to 14 minutes, or until meat near bone is no longer pink and juices run clear, rearranging once. In 1-cup measure, combine glaze ingredients. Microwave at High for 1½ to 2½ minutes, or until mixture boils, stirring once. Arrange chicken on rack in broiler pan. Spoon glaze evenly over chicken. Place under conventional broiler, with surface of meat 6 inches from heat. Broil for 3 to 5 minutes, or until glaze is golden brown. Serve chicken with rice.

Index

Cy DeCosse Incorporated offers
Microwave Cooking Accessories
at special subscriber discounts.
For information write:

Microwave Accessories
5900 Green Oak Drive
Minnetonka, MN 55343